05/17
£2.80

D0830734

Dancing to Learn

Dancing to Learn

Dance as a Strategy in the Primary School Curriculum

Mary Lowden

The Falmer Press

(A Member of the Taylor & Francis Group)
London · New York · Philadelphia

UK   The Falmer Press, Falmer House, Barcombe, Lewes, East Sussex, BN8
              5DL

USA   The Falmer Press, Taylor & Francis Inc., 1900 Frost Road, Suite 101,
              Bristol, PA 19007

© M. Lowden 1989

*All rights reserved. No part of this publication may be reproduced, stored in a
retrieval system, or transmitted, in any form or by means, electronic, mechanical,
photocopying, recording, or otherwise, without permission in writing from the
Publisher.*

First published 1989

**British Library Cataloguing in Publication Data available on
request**

Library of Congress Cataloging-in-Publication Data

Lowden, Mary.
    Dancing to learn : dance as a strategy in the primary school
curriculum / Mary Lowdon.
      p.   cm.
    Bibliography: p.
    Includes index.
    ISBN 1-85000-618-0. — ISBN 1-85000-619-9 (pbk.)
    1. Dancing for children—Study and teaching (Elementary)—Great
Britain. 2. Education, Elementary—Great Britain—Curricula.
I. Title.
GV1799.L68   1989
372.6'6—dc20   89-35947
                                                          CIP

*Printed in Great Britain by Taylor & Francis (Printers) Ltd,
Basingstoke*

Contents

Ideas for Lessons

Dream images

Reality

Acknowledgments

My first debt is to the Brighton Polytechnic education students and tutors with whom I have worked over many years in the exploration and understanding of the arts in school. I am indebted in particular to Kate Fleming for her constant support and inspiration and for permission to use her lesson ideas, especially the lessons about the balance scales, the Good Samaritan, and migration. I am grateful to Les Cross for his sensitive photography and to the schools who gave me the opportunity to work with children, and to photograph their work; in particular David Pratt and Little Common Primary School children, Jan Taylor and Middle Street Primary School children, Angela Mills, Lynda Hills and Meridien Primary School children.

For permission to use copyright material acknowledgement is made to Olwyn Hughes for 'Mushrooms' by Sylvia Plath, which is reprinted by permission of Harper & Row, Inc. 'Water Picture' by Mary Swenson is used by permission of the author, copyright © 1956, renewed © 1984 by Mary Swenson. The poem was first printed in The New Yorker magazine. 'The First Sunrise' is reproduced with kind permission of the authors Elizabeth and John Paynter, © Copyright Universal Edition (London) Ltd.

Introduction

It is hoped that this book will be a valuable support to teachers who already include dance in their teaching, and an inspiration to those who are apprehensive or unaware of the contribution of dance in school.

A central concern of the book is the understanding of the nature of dance. Chapters One and Two attempt to answer the question 'what do children learn in a dance lesson?' and Chapter Three explains how that learning can be planned and implemented. These chapters look at the use of dance within and across the curriculum, not so much as a subject but as a way of coming to know and provide for an understanding that will enable the teacher to identify concepts and abilities to do with other subjects that can be learnt through kinesthetic activity. Language development should provide for various language forms, including dance, if children are to find, formulate, and express their ideas and experiences. Although the language of dance is non-verbal, it is a shared activity and creates a need to talk, in order to consider, explain, argue, direct, suppose, question, describe, and so on. Dance is a way of exploring form and structure and so crosses the bounderies into science and maths and aesthetic appreciation.

Many teachers feel apprehensive about dance because the children are 'loose', because they are not sure how to progress, and because they do not have sufficient understanding to use dance to good purpose. This book provides ideas for practice and explanation of theory and is written in an accessible style in an effort to make dance more available as a learning and teaching tool. Although the book centres on dance in the primary school, the theory is also pertinent to secondary schooling and adult study.

The book is not intended to be read from cover to cover. Theory is cross-referenced with lesson examples and a glossary so that the teacher can bring together dance input, ideas, content, and children's developing abilities, and can find ideas, explanation, and understanding within the context of the teacher's own syllabus and lesson plans. For this reason some of the material is repeated under different sections. The fifty-two lesson examples are not written as recipes but are suggestions intended to spark off ideas and promote alternative ways of interpreting whatever is being discovered or investigated.

The theory and practical ideas are based on many years of teaching dance to children, teachers, and student teachers, and all the lessons have been used in some way. The theory represents my own interpretation of published material and dance study including early training that included Laban's theory of dance in education. Theory and practice is continually being revised and revisited, and for this reason I have stated rather than argued a view based on personal experience that has proved successful yet continually makes necessary the revision of learning and teaching.

1
The Art of Dance

Introduction

In this chapter I show how dance is an art form and as such has a place within the primary school curriculum.

For many people dance means entertainment or social interaction. Dance is disco, tap, and keep fit with jolly music. It is ballroom dance for an evening out and even tea-dance for tea! It is folk, country, or national dance, or ballet in the theatre. Some of this dance is taught in schools, and there are specialist schools that include examinations to show levels of achievement, usually associated with vocational or recreational dance. If we are looking for dance in mainstream education as a contribution to each child's development, we are unlikely to find it in entertainment or social dance, yet in both there are clues to why dance should be included in the school curriculum, and there are certainly clues in ballet.

It goes without saying that all dance is some kind of bodily movement. Movement is also part of our social language by which we are able to communicate with others. We begin to read the language of dance when we interpret everyday bodily movement and posture and when we respond to how bodies look and how they are clothed.

This movement language can be organized in a repeatable and recognizable form which takes on functional significance in situations of formality associated with, for example, government, religion, sport, and law. The movement behaviour and formal clothing of the law court contribute to the importance and stability of law-making itself. They are significant. The church ceremony of marriage with its procession, gestures, costume, flowers, and so on, makes the marriage contract public, extending it into a form in which the significance is shared by the family and guests. In so doing the act itself is given significance.

Significance is the clue to dance in school. Significance is to do with identifying what matters and making that 'mattering' visible or shareable in some way, in other words giving that 'mattering' a significant form.

Dorothy Heathcote describes drama as making ordinary experiences significant and writes:

> In the actual world outside both theatre and school, social events are
> endowed with different degrees of significance. Each social event
> demands variable and selective kinds of ritualised behaviour. These
> different levels, as we acquire understanding of them, become a
> language of social competence by which individuals construe mean-
> ing when amongst others. (Johnson and O'Neill, 1984)

Theatre, ritual, ceremony, pattern, and design are all ways of giving significance to things, events, and objects. It is like putting a magnifying glass on a bit
of life and so giving it special attention, and both the arts and sciences operate
these 'magnifying glasses'. The art form of dance is a way of forming and
sharing the way we respond to the world in which we live by paying particular
attention to experiences, and giving them significance, particularly those
experiences that can be organized and ordered in bodily movement.

It is as an art form that dance has its place on the school timetable.

Sensing and Perception

Making, doing and appreciating any art form brings together two factors, one
being the nature of our environment and the other our perception of it which is
made available to us through our senses.

We pick up and select sensory information according to our sensory
sensitivity and according to our will and interest. Sensory information is
qualitative: light has degrees of intensity and shades of colour; sound has
variations in pitch and volume; space has shape, line, size, and direction. What
we actually see and hear can be measured and recorded. What we actually do
with this information is a very different matter.

Perception is an extension of this sensing. It is a conscious awareness, a
thinking that takes us beyond the realm of what we have sensed and gives us
mastery over our impressions. Through this consciousness we use our senses
to make sense of the world by bringing it under our control, under our will,
and into our interest. We are thus able to do something about the world and
the way we respond to it.

Making sense requires selection and discrimination. The sensory world is
extremely complex and we cannot possibly deal with all the information
available. Selection is dependent upon our frame of reference. We select
according to our purpose, as we do when shopping for a particular meal, or
when we listen to advice. Having selected, we also interpret according to a
particular interest, attitude, or viewpoint. For example, an ammonite picked up
on the beach will mean one thing to a man trying to secure a flimsy belonging
in the wind, and something else to a geologist or historian.

Making sense of the complexity of our outer and inner world depends on
an ability to recognize and organize pattern and relationship. Shaping form,

sequencing pattern, and bringing together different parts in relationships help us to recognize, remember and understand that which is sensed. Art activities provide the opportunity to intentionally explore and create structured images and form compositions; a sequence of notes creates a melody and a rhythm; the structure of two-dimensional shape and colour creates a pictorial statement; a phrase of movement in dance shapes the pathway in space. This ordering of sound, colour, shape, movement, and so on, in fact the exploration and use of any media in arts activities, makes it possible for us to deal with complex and diverse sensations and ideas, and offers a way of dealing with who we are and the kind of environment we live in.

The different art forms provide different experiences of patterning and ordering. A picture is about ordering the lines, shapes, and colour of scene space, images are contained within the space frame although there are examples especially in some oriental pictures and pottery of images that spill over into the imagined space beyond the frame. Except in the imagination, space is empty until it is formed by something that can be seen or touched, and lines and shapes order this space whether it be on a canvas or in the three-dimensional space of sculpture.

The dancer's body and the dancer's movements have a similar effect on the performance space (a more detailed investigation of dance space will be found in Chapter 2). Music is ordered within the beginning and end of its duration, it has a time frame. The form of drama and of dance is framed by the edge of the space that it occupies and by the beginning and end of duration. Dance and drama order time and space.

The formal structure of time in drama is usually ordered by people and events in the drama: people arrive, stay, establish relationships, behave; events have beginnings and consequences and endings and often tell a story. Narrative form is not peculiar to drama or the only form of drama. Narrative form is used in dance, in classical ballets such as 'Les Sylphides', 'Swan Lake', and 'Romeo and Juliet', although in these dances, meaning is also formed by the way space and time is ordered by the movement.

The differences of formal ordering in drama, dance, visual art and music means that one art experience cannot be substituted for another. Each offers a way of dealing with our world that is unique.

Feeling and the Art Activity

Everything we perceive is perceived with feeling. A feeling is a state of mind, and it affects the way in which we cognitively appraise a situation. It is with feeling that we identify and label our response to events, objects and people. Conversely, we understand a felt response through our cognitive apprehension; whether we feel envy or admiration of another's achievement depends upon our cognitive understanding of the situation. That we feel envy may affect that understanding. Feelings illuminate cognition, especially of values, and so affect our judgment, choice, and behaviour; and feelings prompt our action, and determine its substance and direction. Rational thinking, in turn, orders the way we feel, so that we are able to behave appropriately.

Art forming is a way of putting the abstract quality of feeling into a concrete and sensory form. By giving form to felt response we learn to order and formulate the feelings associated with our perceptions and with our sensed information. As a form of feeling the art work is an expression of feeling and to attend to an art work as a creator or spectator is also to attend to the feelings embodied in that work.

As an expression of feeling an art work must not be confused with a symptom of feeling. The art lesson in school is an opportunity for the children to explore feelings. It is not intentional therapy for actual feeling states, although, of course, expression helps individuals to come to terms with their actual feelings and state of mind. To explore feelings, for example, of loneliness, may well involve children talking about their own loneliness but awareness and understanding are the key words, not counselling; exploration of loneliness may help a child to deal with his own experience, but the purpose is to understand the quality, and the context of loneliness itself. A dance study about loneliness might also include investigation about other people's notion of loneliness as expressed for example in art works, in myths and legends, in documentary records. The feeling is explored as a human quality.

Feelings differ according to personal experience and according to different personalities. Art activities provide opportunities for children to compare feelings and expression by exploring other people's responses as well as their own, and so develop an understanding of the relationship between individual feelings and the generally accepted variations of feeling. Personal feelings differ according to the level of concern and point of view in the same way that a sculpture appears different from behind, from in front, or from above. Similarly a dance feels different for the performer than it does for the spectator, and interpretation differs according to experience and ways of looking. A group dance about inside and outside shapes may present the outside shape as protective and liberating while another group of dancers interpret it as a prison preventing escape. So too in real life when a child sees a caring parent as restrictive.

Feelings such as anger, fear, and grief are often expressed clearly in bodily movement which suggests to many teachers that there is a simple equation between emotional expression and making dance. This overlooks the structure and ordering mentioned above, as well as symbolic representation (discussed in Chapter Two). Feelings explored in a context enable the children to go beyond the more primitive feelings of fear and anger, exploring emotions that do not necessarily lead to action in everyday life. Handling the materials of dance leads the children to knowing more about these feelings: for example, in a dance study based on meeting and parting pathways, the different feelings of regret and reconciliation, of anticipation and disappointment are likely to be discovered as a result of changes in speed, distance, and body front; or a group of children create still group statues to express, say, horror, fear, threat, and abhorrence. They are asked to add movement to change from one statue to another and so have to consider the subtle differences of the emotional qualities needed to perform the transitions. The statues and the transitions make it necessary for the children to verbalize and show their understanding of the different meanings in order to clarify the shapes and movements they choose to use.

The act of sharing expression of emotion and feeling through dance encourages the children to examine what they know and believe, and gives them experiences that will help them become more prepared to appreciate what others have to say and feel, as well as interpret and accept new experiences of their own.

Inner feelings and inner thoughts are not valid knowledge as such; we can only really deal with the outward expression of our feelings and thoughts. What we know of feelings is known through action or through the expression of feeling in a concrete form such as the arts provide.

Expression and action in the arts is dependent on the available skills and compositional techniques through which feeling, thought and experience are structured. If we wish to help students to extend their conceptual horizons it is not sufficient simply to offer them extended sensory experience. It is at least equally necessary to help them to a richer *understanding* of the media which gives sense to experience. 'Without the art forms the individual could not have the relevant concepts and therefore the feelings' (Best, 1985).

Creating

Doing any art activity is about making, modifying or developing something. Creativity is not peculiar to the arts, it is a disposition and it relates to any human activity, it is as much to do with science as it is to do with the arts, as much to with work as play, it occurs in thought, action, and feeling, but in school it is probably the arts that most intentionally cater for creative thinking and action.

To be creative is to be innovative, to think and act openly, to be able to put aside the familiar and the safe. It is not only about creating where there was nothing before but also to do with learning about and questioning what is already made. Creativity arises out of having learned the rules and then accepting responsibility for the consequences of questioning them. Creating is as much about making mistakes and about not succeeding as it is about applying successful solutions. It is easy to forget this in school if the emphasis is on the product rather than the process, but it must be remembered that *valid* creativity is dependent to a great extent on skill, experience, and industry. Creativity based solely on immediacy, free of structure, skill, and tradition, is more likely to result in rubbish than art.

In the arts, the process of making is concerned with 'becoming', it involves looking backwards on experience before, during and after the making, it involves forming and looking at the way form becomes ideas, and it continues even beyond the apprehension of the made image. Anticipating, manipulating and realizing are about imagining – imagining what an idea could become, supposing beyond the normally accepted, and dealing with problems in anticipation of their existence. Imagination of this kind is easily suppressed by lack of practice and by ridicule, so that even mistakes and poor skills must be valued and developed constructively. Conversely, imagination is encouraged by sharing: by sharing the imagery of artists in their literature, painting, music, and so on; an imaginative member of a group or an imaginative teacher can spark off the ability or confidence to imagine.

Communication

Art works communicate. They are statements that can be read by touching, looking, and listening. Art works are communication but have no fixed meanings nor recipes for making or reading their meanings. Each art image has its own articulation according to the organization of materials that constitute the form; each is a statement, not a translation of a statement. A dance is a dance, not a message.

The reference for making and reading an art work is one's own reality, so that what the spectator sees may not be the same as what the artist intended, and two spectators may have two different interpretations according to their own experience of reality. Meaning in the arts is also dynamic; it is not fixed but provides an infinite range of possible interpretations. Nevertheless, each art work deals with an aspect of reality with which the materials and the compositional devices have an affinity without which sharing and communication would not be possible.

In created images that closely resemble reality and are very literal, the interpretation is fixed according to that reality, as it is perceived, but it is the nature of art activity that each moment of perception sets off another image and another thought so that the artist and the spectator continually move into the contemplation of the possible.

A dance lesson that explores the changing shape of autumn leaves will not only be about leaves, it may set off ideas about change, decay, death, group shape, interpersonal relationships, and the cycle of birth and rebirth.

In dance, music, and drama, communication and sharing are a necessary part of the process of the composition. Apart from sharing oneself as an instrument of expression, the sharing of work and the opportunity to look at the work of others includes making aesthetic and artistic judgments. The aesthetic is not synonymous with the artistic. Like creativity, the aesthetic can occur in all aspects of life and can apply to any object and to any activity. To say that a picture is beautiful may mean it is beautiful both artistically and aesthetically, but to say that a tree is beautiful is not to say it is a beautiful work of art. An artist may deliberately challenge accepted aesthetic conditions and choose to take little note of accepted aesthetic significance. She may intentionally horrify and visually disturb so that the art work is anything but aesthetic. There is however a close relationship between aesthetic and artistic appraisal and artistic appreciation. Art-making is concerned with the nature and expression of form so that art activity and art appreciation are likely to involve children in activities that include the appraisal of both the aesthetic and the artistic.

Making Judgments

Aesthetic judgment occurs whenever form is contemplated. It is about giving attention to form, being aware of positive and negative qualities, and apprehending meaning through attention to the significance of form. A found pebble on a beach could be the object of aesthetic contemplation so that its colour, texture, size and shape are valued for the way these qualities occur and are related to the form of the pebble. The way a thing is results from what it is; form and function are close partners. A chair is for sitting on and the success of its shape is related to its success as piece of sitting-on furniture. Likewise a dance appraisal must include its purpose if that is significant: a dance to entertain must be entertaining.

Judgment can be subjective, concerned with liking or not liking and based only on feelings of preference. Preference may be prompted by a lack of information as much as by being informed; judgments can be made according to irrelevant and inappropriate influences; they can be based on prejudice and lack of experience. What matters in learning is that children develop the ability to make judgments that are supported by reasons and which therefore support the development of understanding based on rational and informed judgment. Because knowledge colours judgment it is not always possible, or indeed desirable, to distinguish between subjective preference and rational judgment, but those who teach must be able to make judgments that they can substantiate and enable children to do the same.

Aesthetic judgment is a value judgment that is likely to be influenced by moral values. Intrinsically good often refers to something that is life-upholding, whereas intrinsically bad refers to something that is life-destroying, thus erotic is good, pornography is bad; harmony and balance is good, discord and being out of rhythm is bad.

Artistic appraisal is about techniques and structure, and about the interaction between the media and content, although an art work, from the aesthetic point of view, is rather like the pebble: it is something contemplated for its own sake. An art work is expressive, communicative, it has form and content and is contemplated as a whole. It is doubtful whether artistic appreciation of one art form can be transferred to another, but the ability to recognize and appraise aesthetic qualities is developed through immersion in aesthetic phenomena and it is the arts activities that are most likely to provide opportunities for this immersion.

Artistic sensitivity and the degree of aesthetic response can only be assessed when it is evident. This means that judgment cannot depend on subjective hunches but must be supported by an objective rationale based on evidence in the process or the final product. The appraisal of bodily skill in dance must be based on actual skilful performance, sensitive use of colour in visual art must be demonstrated by the way colour is used, the understanding and investigation of content and meaning must be based on the way that content is dealt with in the work. The artist makes concrete and public what she knows and feels through the work and it is on this that understanding is judged.

Appraisal of art work in school is not quite the same as the appraisal of a work in the theatre or art gallery. Appraisal in school is also concerned with the way a child is developing, and should take into account abilities, attitudes, and experiences. This appraisal will include considerations such as level of commitment, social sensitivity, the ability to be verbally articulate about the work, realization of potential ability, and the kind of experiences that are available to the child. The nature of participation itself is significant and the teacher must make use of any opportunity to observe the children working, and discuss their work with them. Listening to the way a group of children create a group dance might give more clues about their understanding than the actual dance. Having said that, the ultimate objective is that the work itself must stand alone. Discussion may explain or excuse, but eventually the art work is the object of appraisal.

Conclusion

In conclusion I can do no better than quote Gordon Curl (ATCDE Lecture 1971) and pass on his suggestion of a kind of catechism for dance educators, a catechism prompted by Karl Popper's belief in three worlds; a world of physical bodies, animate and inanimate, a world of conscious experience, feelings and perceived qualities, and a world of symbolic forms, theories and knowledge:

> such a pluralist position ... may help the dance educator to recognize more clearly the autonomous nature of the dance dimension as symbolic activity and its intricate web of relations with movement as its material and its perceived quality as its medium (Christmas Conference 1971 ATCDE, University of London).

For the same reason this chapter and the following one take apart the art-making process, but it is essential that the parts are understood in order to grasp the whole, in order to make good teaching theory into good learning practice, and to interact between experience, reality and the expression of reality to make good art.

2
Dance Education and Dance in Education

Introduction

The arts in education contribute to learning in two ways. The first is about the development of the child in general and the second is about the child's artistic ability and understanding. In any learning activity it may be impossible and even unnecessary to distinguish between the two, since they continually fuse and complement each other, reflecting the synthesis of experience in all learning.

So when is an art lesson about learning to draw, and when is it about the observation of a fossil? When is social interaction in drama about learning to work with others, and when about social relationships within theatre? When is dance about creating opposing forces, and when about the bodily management of space? In planning and doing the arts activity it may be difficult to identify the kind of learning that is really taking place, but the teacher must identify the main thrust of the lesson in order to structure the learning, to develop particular skills, and to evaluate or build on achievement. The dance teacher must understand the nature of dance and the kind of learning that it involves and makes possible.

What is it that a child learns when dance is included in the timetable, and what is lacking when there is no provision for dance? Dance is social and physical, but learning to socialize is not dependent on dance, and neither are physical skill and fitness, or problem-solving, or being creative. In this chapter I show how dance orders space, time and energy using the body as the instrument, and examine dance as a language. Having examined the nature of dance I then look at its contribution within the curriculum.

Space

In dance the movement of the body makes the space visible and therefore communicable. The body is three-dimensional, so that dance deals with volume, with up and down, with left and right, with forward and backward, with pathways and gesture. Other curriculum activities also include spatial experience: geometry is about shape and space, but is often represented on two-dimensional paper; in sculpture and clay work the child forms three-dimensional shapes, but in fixed forms. It is in dance that the child experiences the relationship between one dimension and another, including the change or making of shape through time.

In dance the shaping of space is seen. It is experienced as mass, as projection, and as tension in space. In reality objects and the spaces between them are still, shapes of things have edges and mass, a mass that can be captured in sculpture and even in still moments in a dance: when bodies are still in dance, they are sculpture-like.

A dancer travelling in space creates a pathway on the floor following the feet or in the air following the body or parts of the body, and this is spatial progression. As the body progresses through space the spectator can follow the pathway of the movement, as with a sparkler. Because this takes time, imagination and anticipation is brought into play to bring together the beginning, middle and end as a coherent whole.

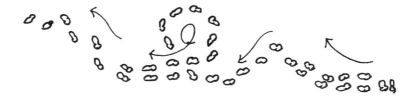

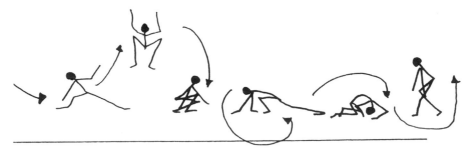

Empty space can be filled with tension like the tension that can be physically felt between the like and unlike poles of a magnet. This energy can be created by a movement that sends off energy into the space. It can be created by a single dancer in relation to an object or in relation to the empty space ... as a church spire informs the infinite above, so a dancer can inform the space beyond the body.

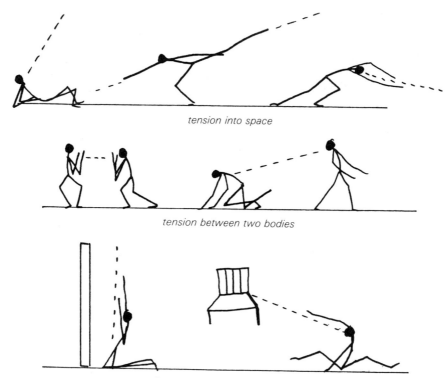

tension into space

tension between two bodies

tension between a body and an object

By moving in and around space, the dancer can contain space. Space can be held, confined, protected, even cherished. To encircle a space is to give it a specialness, and is evident in ritual and sacred rites; to dance around a centre is to maintain a constant relationship with the centre, with the source of the centre, perhaps with the source of life itself. To cup space in the hands is to protect or imprison the space within the hands, a curving arm can gather together space, a spreading arm opens up the space and lets in an emptiness.

the arms containing space

Figure 1   Describing the kind of space that is occupied. The body can appear crushed and squashed as if space were too small for the body.

The dancer can use actions and movement shape to describe the kind of space that is being occupied, the body can appear crushed and squashed as if space was too small for the body, it can reach and stretch as if space were unlimited.

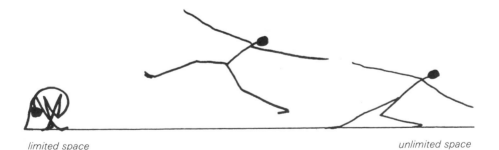

limited space   *unlimited space*

Much tension can be created in a space by what surrounds it: imagine the feel of a space surrounded by a circle of dancers intently focusing on the centre, or imagine the space between two strongly opposed groups, a space filled with the power of hatred, antagonism, opposition.

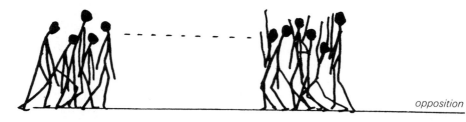

opposition

A dance space, as with space in everyday life, is usually occupied by more than one dancer, so that the shapes of space overlap or are shared. Dancers can appear to guard their space, or weave between others, or fuse their kinetic space with that of others. What happens spontaneously in crowded places also happens in the dance space, but intentionally.

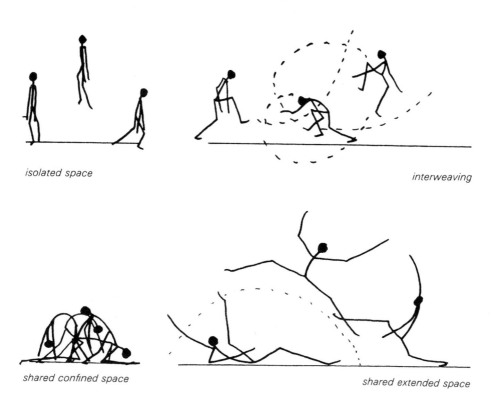

isolated space

interweaving

shared confined space

shared extended space

Space can be held off as if it were an intruder and unwanted, it can be pushed away with the hands or ignored by turning one's back or averting the eyes. The dancer can set up a relationship with the space as if it were evil and threatening by avoiding places and by keeping to the outside edge. Other people's body space can be treated in the same way so that the people too are seen to be rejected or threatened by the dancer's movement.

15

Mary Lowden

Time

The dancer's movement orders time and makes visible the temporal qualities of duration, speed, and sequence. The length of a dance or movement study is related to the content, to structure and dance ability, and to the demands of strenuous movement. Theatre performances last about an hour or less, and an evening's programme frequently consists of three dances, each of forty minutes' duration, with two intervals. In school dance or movement study, two or three minutes is often long enough for the children's ideas and span of concentration.

The contribution of passages of stillness and silence in dance and in music is often overlooked for fear that inactive children are uncontrolled or unoccupied. Pauses of considered length within the context of the dance work will encourage concentration and create an opportunity for the children to develop ideas sensitively and create meaning.

Although stillness is motionless it has a given time, it has energy and occupies space within the dance form. Stillness, and silence in music are not a cessation, but a quality of movement or of sound, with meaning given by duration and place in the sequence, and a quality given by their place and relationship within the context. A still body can project tension, can be withdrawn, can embrace the space around or be shut in. How the body became still and how the stillness is resolved gives meaning to the stillness in the same way that a gesture informs the gestures that follow and precede it.

Between the beginning and end of any action there is a passage of time. Some actions seem to only occupy time, like making a cup of tea, waiting, or travelling on a journey. A dance does more than occupy time, it forms time. The duration of time is given significance by the way the body moves, by dynamic qualities of force and speed, and by the temporal complexity of rhythm which affects the feel of that time-span. An everyday example is the feeling of hurrying when we are short of time and have to move quickly, or dawdling when we have time to spare. Words like 'hurry', 'rush', 'bustle', 'loiter', and 'dawdle', describe the emotion of fastness or the emotion of slowness as do the movements in dance. The quality of time is felt, not measured. Acceleration and deceleration of speed are expressed as feeling states: acceleration expresses a climax, increasing excitement, a gathering together of force, a culmination; deceleration can express fatigue, change of heart, growing disappointment, parting or coming to an end, fading away.

Rhythm is time patterned by repeated changes between two elements, one ·strong and one weak, and it is the movement between these two that sets up the rhythm. Rhythm is created by a change of intensity. Changes in the gravitational pull of the moon set the rhythm of the tides; the rotation of the earth sets up the rhythm of day and night.

It is the preparation of a new event by the ending of the previous one
... it is the setting up of new tensions by the resolution of former ones.

16

They need not be of equal duration but the situation that begets the old crisis must be inherent in the dénoument of the forerunner. (Langer, 1953).

This relationship between the new and the past event is experienced continuously in the exhalation and inhalation of breath, and indeed Doris Humphrey's dance style was based on the movement flow of the rise and fall of breathing, the intake of breath as a renewal of energy as the body lifts and falls.

Rhythm is a quality of temporal order. Man as he lives in the world is continuously exposed to rhythmic phenomena in the environment and in his own body, and the rhythmic patterns available to man are those learnt within his own experience. As a feature of the environment and of organic matter rhythm is a fact, as a feature of making dance it is an idea based on that reality.

In western music and dance the principle of rhythm is division. Time is divided into parts to give it structure and to give it a recognizable order that can be sensed and remembered. This division is based on the idea of quantity and quality, on how much and how long.

A length of time
_____

divided
_____   _____

_____   _____   _____   _____

___ ___   ___ ___   ___ ___   ___ ___

The division of time is organized in two ways according to stress:

(1) Duple time: ∧ — ∧ — written as 2/4 time;
(2) Triple time: ∧ − − ∧ − − written as 3/4 time.

In music, time values have note equivalents and are notated thus:

$\bf{o}$ = 1 semibreve
♩♩ = 2 minims
♩♩♩♩ = 4 crotchets
♪♪♪♪♪♪♪♪ = 8 quavers.

Music notation divides the duration into bars, which are usually of equal length so that the time values of each bar are equal.

The primary division of duple time is two or four beats, and of triple time three beats. The time signature at the begining of a piece of music gives these values, for example 2/2 time is two minims in a bar, 3/4 time is three crotchets in a bar. Nearly all time variations are based on these two common times, for example, the compound time of 6/8 is six quavers or two dotted crotchets, the dot representing a value of half the preceeding note.

In western music and dance the duple and triple time is so fixed that it is usually the starting point of any rhythmic experience. When music is constantly used in a dance lesson, movements are likely to comply with this fixed measurement of time.

It is possible that 2/4 and 3/4 time originated from the sound rhythms created by dancers wearing beads or bells, or by workers singing as they worked. The specific time values probably derive from the metric beat of the human step action and/or the pulse of the heart beat.

The notation of notes of fixed values in music make it possible for composers to write music that they do not play and for interpreters to play music that they have not created. The effect of this separation between performer and composer is that the theoretical knowledge becomes distinct from the practical knowledge and explains why of all the arts music is the most concerned with instrumental skill and theoretical instruction. Rhythm systems in dance are also well established and it was the influence of dance and music that changed the free rhythms of early plainsong to the steady two, three, or four beat. Thoinot Arbeau's dancing manual of 1589 gives a strict rule for stepping and playing an instrument:

> A single pace contains five feet which would make two thousand to a league. As the drum beats the rhythm of one step, each step is the beat of the minim. It follows that the two crotchets or four quavers equal one minim of a step.

Folk dance, ballroom dance, classical ballet, pop and disco dance use these same minim beats. It is the recurrent accent that accounts for the excitement of rhythm and its effect on the emotions. The changing force between the accent and non-accent when maintained continuously sets up an accord with the peripheral sense receptors of the nervous system which produces an automatic response and body feeling that is controlled by the rhythm. This is why relayed factory music maintains the work rhythms and military band music keeps the soldiers marching. This automatic response and induced excitement explains the appeal of pop music and pop dance.

Dance also has rhythm within its composition. Just as day and night or the change of the seasons is rhythmic, the events in a dance (or a story, or a play), set up a rhythmic pattern, an excitement, like the repetition of Goldilock's adventures which creates the build-up of anticipation. Repeated movements and phrases of movement enable the dancer, and, more importantly, the spectator, to become familiar with certain passages which creates a sense of ownership and makes possible surprise when the pattern is broken, and climax when it is accelerated.

Recurrent movements or phrases do not have to conform to rules of frequency, they can be irregular and represented by uneven states of tension or resolution which nonetheless contribute to the rhythm of the whole. A gesture such as an arm encircling, or the flow of a movement phrase, creates a periodicity of time and spatial rhythm, and once this is established it can be played upon by changing the space, place, time, and body part. Although the movement takes on a different quality the composition is recognizable by the spectator because he has, as it were, been tutored in the initial rhythm.

The conscious development, manipulation, and creation of rhythm can be facilitated by marking the rhythm with counts or written marks as in notation. For example, beginning with a free stepping pathway:

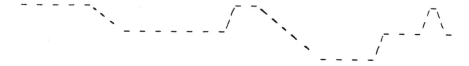

add a regular change of direction:

count in an accent and a change in accent:

and a change in the rhythm:

The accurate performance of this stepping sequence might require careful counting, but counting should retain the sensed experience of the rhythm. A conductor or choreographer in control of time does this by bodily feeling the rhythm; it is almost impossible to make rhythmic sound without moving.

Figure 2   The felt rhythm of jumping.

Whether children are exploring free or metric rhythm, the experience must be a sensed experience. It is essential that children 'catch' the rhythm through body movement, not only in dance but in music and in physical activities that are rhythmic such as running and throwing. The felt rhythm of work actions, of instrumental performance, and of functional movement contributes to efficient management of the action and of the energy used. Rhythm is not a conscious intellectual activity although its development and application might become so. Jazz, blues, rock and roll, even the very complex rhythms of West African drumming, are bodily felt, and counting and notating are neither possible nor desirable. Walking, swinging arms, jumping, nodding, turning and rolling, swaying, falling and standing, tapping — these are rhythm, and doing them is a rhythmic experience.

Sequence

The dancer experiences and performs the passage of time by filling it with movements that precede and follow. Movements are sequentially ordered according to the content and structure of the dance. When children make and join sequences of movement they become involved in this ordering, and structure arrangements and make choices based on logical and rational reasoning, reasoning that takes into account aesthetics, meaning, and management. Swopping sections of a dance can help children discover the difference between introductory material and material that is developing ideas or bringing them to a conclusion. Composition can be explored by repeating sequences and adding variations. The search for a good ending for a dance might entail a review of all that has gone before to identify the way ideas unfold and to bring the piece to an appropriate finish. As children edit and refine their work so they come to recognize inappropriate material and ideas that are out of sequence.

This sequencing in movement also makes visible the passing of time. The relationship between the past and the future can be emphasized in a single movement phrase, as when a dancer crosses the space and changes the focus from the point of departure to the point of arrival. If within such a phrase changes of shape or social interaction occur, then the audience see the difference between the past and the present, and the dancer can make visible cause and effect, action and reaction, or recurring phenomena.

in touch with the past   *in the present*   *in touch with the future*

Non-stop movement, sequences that pass rapidly from one group to another, many groups dancing at the same time, and complex rhythms pack a lot of material into a short time as if time was squeezed up together. Likewise time can be stretched, elongated; gestures that are very sustained create an illusion of lengthened time. This may also be created by extending the amount of space so that a gesture will seem to go on and on into space as well as into time. Real time, although measured in minutes and hours, can also feel condensed or protracted: a day in a hospital can feel like a week, three hours of exciting activity can seem like five minutes.

Temporal experience is part of everyday life and includes physical behaviour: the children will know about suddenly withdrawing a hand, rushing about in a panic, waiting and more waiting. They bring these experiences to the lesson, but need the opportunity to develop and formulate the experiences so that the qualities become conscious, notable and imagined, and so become 'a free symbolic form which may be used to convey ideas of emotion, of awareness and premonition' (Langer, 1958).

Awareness comes from watching, from making, and from evaluating, and should be supported by talk, drawing, and writing. Simple notation symbols can contribute to this awareness and extend the ability to use the management of time and space as an instrument of creating dance.

The following notation shows:

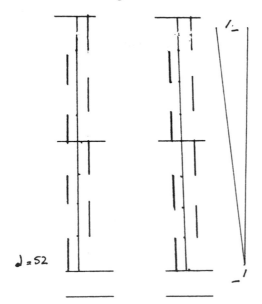

two bars of four counts, stepping action increasing speed, a beat of 52 beats per minute.

In school dance children are likely to find the right duration and tempo for their expression and ability through *doing* dance. Dance education seldom uses notated scores as music does, but recorded music is frequently used to direct the time qualities. Be aware that if you rely on music, the sound directs and prescribes the rhythm, phrase, duration, and sequence, and because music is expressive it also prescribes the mood and style of the action.

Energy: The Vitality of Dance

Energy, force, weight, effort, power. These are words used to describe what makes the body move, to describe the power of energy, and the effect of that power on the quality of the movement. The body is the dance instrument and it is the movement of that instrument that makes the structure and form of dance available to the senses. That movement is powered by body energy, it is the force with which we locomote, act, breathe, pump oxygen round the body, and resist the downward pull of gravity. The way in which that force is used in dance and non-verbal communication colours expression so that a gesture or a body action also show the feelings of the mover.

The quality of force also controls and is controlled by skill, technique, will, emotion, and attitude. In dance such control is used to manage the body energy in order to create movement images of meaning, it is used to free that energy, to free it right through to the finger-tips or toes into the space beyond the performance space. The dancer learns to manage that energy efficiently, using it to elevate the body, to balance, and to sustain energy. This management is a fusion of imagination and physics, so that incurling the spine from a dropped position is facilitated by imagining a downward thrust of energy through the legs as well as understanding the structure of the spine; a confident and accurate posture is attained by imagining tallness and knowing about alignment. Using as an example the ordinary but often mimed action of threading a needle we can see that the force used to thread a needle is not calculated but sensed according to the thread, the eye of the needle, the light, the sensitivity of the fingers, the position of the body, the environment. In everyday actions we are able to select movements appropriate to the task, and practise new tasks to find the right movement qualities. How a movement is performed is affected by intentions, skills, communication, emotion, information and context. A dance movement is all this plus the imagination to interpret and explore the idea in an imagined context.

The way different circumstances and attitudes influence the quality of a movement means that there is no single way of encouraging a child to find an expressive movement; a way of moving up from the floor might be found by considering which bit moves first, imagining the body is pulled up by a puppet master, imitating the image of a rope hauling up a load, using a feeling of unwillingness, responding to music or poetry. The sensation of movement and the varied experiences that colour its performance are tools for the teacher.

The sensing and awareness of force can be found by actually lifting and carrying objects or pushing and pulling heavy and light furniture. Children might try lifting a heavy stone and then a paper tissue, followed by lifting the tissue as if it were stone. This kind of exercise explores the sensation in reality

23

Figure 3 Sensing movements appropriate for the task; the amount of force to thread a needle.

and then in the imagination: there is a need to refer to reality to find the imaginable. Pushing against the wall of the classroom is not at all the same movement as *pretending* to push against a wall because the resistance is imagined, but the experience helps the child to 'feel' the wall, to 'feel' the movement, and to 'feel' the circumstance of pushing against a wall, just as drawing from still life enables the artist to express depth and distance with drawing materials. In another exercise, a group of children might pass a chair from one to another in turn to find out about timing, placing, and degree of force, then build on this real experience to imagine that the chair is ... a time bomb, on ostrich egg, or contraband. The same movements performed without a chair enable the children to extract and abstract the movement ideas, to see the effect of speed or of rhythm on the energy, to play with the ideas and so create dance movements. Ideas based on this exercise might lead to a dance study about refugees or work and shared labour.

The dance is made real by the energy of the body — this is the force and power of dance. This vitality is a powerful medium, it is a primitive power and in early civilizations was an essential part of life associated with magic, spiritual transcendence, religious fervour, ecstasy and war. This physical activity was a way of man controlling and understanding himself and the environment. Although dance is now an activity of thought and reasoning and school dance a lesson on the timetable, body movement still has this power of energy and force, as is evident in pop dance, in military processions, and in football crowds swaying and singing. This power is also there to a lesser degree in the dance lesson and explains why some teachers are apprehensive; if used well it is a power for motivation, self-confidence and achievement.

The Body as an Instrument

The space and time of dance is given form and meaning through bodily movement, the body being the means whereby the space and time on the dancer's 'canvas' is organized. The way the body is used to think and imagine in dance must be understood in order to differentiate that use from other activities that use physical skills.

Increased ability to manage the body develops the sense of personal awareness, an awareness in dance that contributes to self-awareness and a confidence in one's self-image. This is one reason why parents send their children to ballet classes. This bodily awareness is developed to a very fine level by the professional dancer who can perform complex and finely balanced placements in rapid succession, accurately repeat them, and confidently fill a stage space.

I am not suggesting that school dance should begin with exercises at the bar, but it is important to provide the opportunity for children to consciously dwell on this body sensing, which may be done by simply lying on the floor.

25

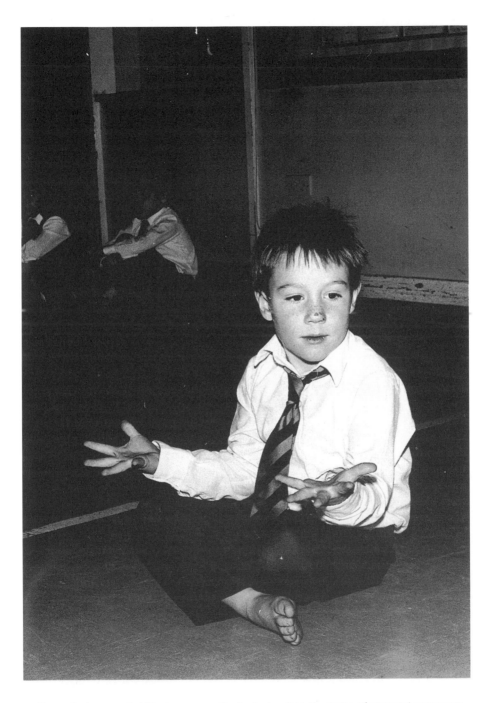

Figure 4   Increased ability to manage the body develops the sense of personal awareness.

The children will have bodily sensations about the pressure of the floor and the giving way to gravity, they will bodily sense the shape and position of legs and arms and experience feelings that are associated with the placing and shape of the body.

Lying quietly or standing still in order to focus on this sensing is a sensitive activity and takes time. A cold gymnasium floor which doubles as a corridor is not conducive to this sensing; neither is wearing underclothes when it is cold, or when it is warm for that matter, because they suggest and make necessary energetic activity. What the children wear and where they do dance depends on the content of the lesson and the nature of the experience. What is often considered normal practice is often irrational. Is it logical to take off shoes to protect the floor when shoes are worn on the same surface for dinner or assembly? Is it really safer without shoes? Are bare feet always the most suitable footwear? What about making rhythmic step patterns using the sound of footsteps? Clean wellington boots and outdoor coats could be wonderful costume and stimulus for travelling on an imaginative journey. Body awareness can be a quiet, sensitive affair and as necessary as leaps and jumps. Awareness is the key word, so consider the hall space. Is it the best space? How about developing sensitive body awareness by sitting on a chair or lying on the story-time carpet?

Body Thinking, Body/Mind Feeling

Traditionally our cultural background persuades us that the body and mind are separate, and certainly there is much evidence to support this theory. Physical activities are more public than mental activities, the mind can function 'energetically' without using apparent physical energy, and there are bodily activities that appear to be little associated with thinking at all!

A dualist view tends to regard the mind as being superior to the body, a view that is implicit in school timetables and in many methods of assessment. It is implied in a primary school where Maths and English are timetabled for the morning session and the more physically active lessons are 'permitted' when children have completed their 'real work'. It is implied when children are 'excused' from classroom 'work' to practise their dance, drama and music Christmas performance and left to work alone with little or no direction or planned development.

All learning is about thinking. So where does thinking happen? In the head! So it would seem when we do mental arithmetic or ponder problems. But consider an artist making a pencil drawing of a rose. She closely observes the information in front of her, not only visually, but sensing the quality of the form, taking into account also an experience of roses and gardens and maybe cultivating them. She may have to touch the flower or take another rose apart to examine and understand the structure and feel of the rose, so collecting information that informs the perception. She draws, and it is as if the pencil point itself searches for understanding and deals with problems of distance and light to discover the essential nature of the rose. The drawing is a thought process. If the mind is anywhere it is in the point of the pencil or in the hand that guides the pencil! Similarly with the potter moulding clay, a good pot might have a balanced shape, significant patterning and a knowledgable attention to function. The proportion, size, and weight are well considered, they are thought about and searched for and found with the hands.

So how does the dancer think? Creating dance theoretically on paper is, with a few exceptions, neither practicable nor possible. It is necessary to think about the shape and rhythm of the movement whilst either being in one's own body or having someone else's body to work with. A movement such as a hand gesture can communicate a variety of meanings: offering or asking for help, friendship, need or generosity; the intended meaning and the performance of that gesture is considered and selected according to how the image looks and feels, thinking about structure and meaning is done with the body.

Although the above example is a simple one, the understanding and acceptance of bodily thought has philosophical implications. If we accept that we can think with the body, and value the development of thought as part of the educational process, it follows that we must respect the thinking that happens in dance, and value the contribution of bodily activity in coming to know. Such understanding could give dance a more prominant place in the timetable. The day's programme could begin with dance as a way of exploring shape in the maths lesson, and language work include movement as a vital element in communication.

The acceptance of movement as a thinking process also means that thought actions such as selecting, finding schematics, seeing connections, making judgments, assessing a problem, and applying a solution should be evident in the dance lesson. An activity that is concerned only with recognizable movements and acceptable values and feelings runs the risk of producing a product of some sort that might even appear admirable, yet be fairly mindless. Dress twenty children in crêpe paper, train them to move in unison and recite a few lines of poetry and there is an acceptable morning assembly about spring! Any activity, including assembly and Christmas performances, must be concerned with the level of thinking if the activity matters, if it is justifiable as a school activity.

One of the exciting things about teaching dance is that the teacher can 'see' the children's thought processes. A group of children are asked to explore the difference between gradual and sudden contrasts of speed. As they work the teacher can see how much the children understand about contrast, slowness and fastness, how much help they need and whether the task is sufficiently challenging. The level of thinking is evident in the way the children sort out their problems and put together the dance work.

The Language of Dance

The gestures and postures of the body are felt utterances, though often not consciously so, and are rooted in instinctive behaviour. Folding the arms in front of the body protects the vulnerable soft parts from, say, cold wind or something dangerous like thrown stones. As a gesture it appears to shut out not danger, but other people, enclosing the body in the safety of the self. A teacher with folded arms is thus protected from the children who instinctively respond as if excluded. An open hand offered in friendship is both a sign and attitude of friendship and understandable as such.

In one accepted sense of language, signs and symbols are artificial and contribute to methods of control that are conscious. Numerical figures enable us to calculate and measure; cartography symbols help us to view a large portion of the countryside the better to plan and construct roads or bridge rivers. The artificial symbols of words, 'cat', 'object', 'tomorrow', 'small', enable us to discriminate and classify and communicate. Increased artificiality in language forms provides for abstraction and makes it possible to deal with things beyond our immediate reality, making what is unconscious, conscious.

Dance also has its artificial symbols that function as conventional signs that are agreed in order to be understood. In the language of Indian dance, for example, there are rigid rules for the gestural hand signs.

Figure 5   The gestures and postures of the body are felt utterances and are rooted in instinctive behaviour.

> The language for the hands in Hast–Mudras is the most beautiful in
> the complexity of symbolism. The hand position in which the thumb
> is bent across the outstretched fingers expresses such things as the
> beginning of the dance, clouds, woods, river, night, bravery and
> sparkling water. (Walter Sorell, 1967)

Another example in dance is the mime actions of the Commedia dell'Arte,
some of which have been absorbed into the language of classical ballet.
Rudolph Laban's spatial organization in movement attempts to define 'rules of
grammar of the language of movement'. These are clusters of choreutic units
which combine to create a logical and articulate form, to create dance, and to
analyze its form and meaning.

School dance is not necessarily concerned with a specific body language,
but it does deal with meanings that can be communicated through movement
because the movement used and the body articulation has an affinity with
qualities and form in real situations, meanings that are suggested by association
rather than specified. Thus the folding of the arms has an affinity with
protection, and unfolding an affinity with increase in size and openness; a rising
movement has an affinity with verticality and weightlessness, a sinking
movement with giving in to gravity, with giving way, with heaviness and
fatigue.

Body language is part of the here and now of reality, the gestures and
postures are products of real situations, of real feelings and sensed experience,
but may be intentionally used to stand for and represent reality. The following
is a description of how this operates:

> A subjective attitude of anger is expressed in a face to face confron-
> tation through facial expression, aggressive gesture and posture,
> which enables me to read how the other person feels. The angry
> person may further express his anger by using a knife. If I find that
> knife stuck in the wall above my head although the adversary is
> absent, I feel fear because the knife stands for his anger. Similarly, the
> facial expression and body posture are products of the human
> activity. I may take these selfsame products and intentionally use
> them to stand for and represent anger, so that the knife or the gesture
> are signs and symbols for anger, a sign shared by others and
> commonly accepted, which can be used to objectively communicate
> anger. (Bergman and Luckman, 1971).

Gestures that recognizably represent reality are more evident in drama
than in dance. It is possible to place a dramatized situation in a real context so
that the drama appears as if real. Take a dramatized scene in which a lover bids
a fond farewell to his loved one as she departs on a journey; enact that same
scene at a railway station and it could be accepted as real. Although there are
exceptions, the danced interpretation of the same scene is likely to include
formulated gestures of farewell in a dance-like way, adding, say, notable
changes of speed and extended pathways and repetition. The scene danced on a

railway station would be either an embarrassment or an entertainment! The language of dance uses formalized actions that are abstractions of real ideas and situations, and appear more distanced from reality than drama, but however real the 'as if' nature of drama appears, the signs and symbols of speech and movement in drama are not real, they stand for reality as they do in dance, the difference being that drama frequently deals with social situations as they actually exist.

As well as using signs and symbols to deal with reality, language can transcend the reality of everyday life through symbolism by using the experience of one situation to refer to another. Hamlet's contemplation of suicide is an example:

O, that this too too solid flesh would melt,
Thaw and resolve itself into a dew,
Or that the everlasting has not fixed
His cannon 'gainst self slaughter,

How weary, flat, stale and unprofitable
Seem to me all the uses of this world!
Fie ont! O fie, 'tis an unweeded garden
That grows to seed, things rank and gross in nature
Possess it merely.

By symbolism I mean anything that stands for something else, including sign, metaphor, myth, legend, instrumental sound, stories, and words. Religions and all art forms are symbolic forms and also contain within them many kinds of symbolism.

Take, for example, the classical ballet 'Swan Lake'. The symbolic *form* is dance; the symbolic compositional *device* is a legend; the subject is the transformation of mortal life; and the symbolic *image* is a swan. The story of 'Swan Lake' takes place in the romantic setting of dusk, forest, and lake. The swan and its gliding motion is a symbol of beauty also epitomized in the 'S' curve of the swan's neck. Immortality is symbolized in the ethereal weightlessness of the dancer, innocence and dream is captured by a costume of white feathers, and the unattainable represented by the fading away of something beautiful.

A symbolic image can be used to recall sensed experiences. Words, music, smells, sounds, scenes and bodily sensations can bring into mind feelings and thoughts associated with an event, situation, or relationship, and so colour the image. In the following lines from T.S. Eliot's *Waste Land*, it is the association with smell that colours the image.

You gave me hyacinths first a year ago
They called me the hyacinth girl
Yet when we came back from the hyacinth garden
Your arms full and your hair wet, I
Could not speak....

31

The sensed experience of smell is particularly associated with memory. The hyacinth has a strong smell so that the reader colours the lines of the poem with memory evoked by the mention of hyacinths. In dance, the recall of sensed experience and associated memory often refers to seeing or experiencing body sensations that have associations with situations, like seeing someone rocking in grief or hiding the face to shut out something unpleasant, or having experienced the intoxication of moving in time to a strong rhythm. The picture image of the harshness of the crown of thorns in Robert Cohan's dance 'Stabat Mater' is not only represented by the dance movements and staccato music, but is associated with the physical memory of sharply pointed objects and stabbing actions so that the spectator's experience contributes to the danced image of cruelty and suffering of Christ's crucifixion.

Symbolism formulates experience into something imaginable enabling us to be more articulate about experience. Primary school activities make possible and encourage the interaction between different subjects and should make it very possible for the children to explore and use a variety of symbolic images that cross subject bounderies encouraging the children to imagine differently and to order experience differently so widening their conceptual understanding.

Consider the different symbol systems used in the following example. A class of children investigate shells and creatures in shells. They measure the shell markings and classify the species. Drawings are made of various shell forms focusing on the relationship between the inside and outside. Using the drawings the children create inside and outside shapes in clay and use language to describe the function and relationship. The drawings, measurements and clay models are reference for a group dance about containing and being contained. Children create music and spoken poetry to accompany the dance study. Drawings are used to make overhead slides as a setting for the dance and music.

These different symbol images make it possible to investigate, record, calculate, communicate and formulate understanding differently, bringing together and respecting the particular subject disciplines and modes of working. Thus the children have dealt with the reality of the shells and become aware and informed about shells, and can articulate their response, develop associated ideas, and share what they know with others.

Theme and topic based activities in school frequently focus on the actual and measurable reality of the content or subject matter rather than the different modes of learning or interpretation. A topic such as the example above may then be little more than a collection of samples and drawings to illustrate a day's outing to the sea, and what is seen as a scheme of work is nothing more than an assembling of materials. It is what the children do with information and experience that matters. Having identified the topic or project content, teachers must ask questions about how the children respond, what the experience meant to the children, how the meaning was developed, and whether the experience and method of working was appropriate and worthwhile.

In giving form to interpretation, the children's dance, music, clay and poetry images in the shell example do more than stand for the nature of the shells or inside and outside phenomena. What is represented is their interpretation, their curiosity, and their understanding, which also exists and becomes formed in the art image so that the work takes on its own reality. Although the above example began with real shells, the drawings and movements, sounds and words, develop the children's ideas. The children become involved in pattern, in shape, in the marvel of the natural world, in their own feeling and ideas about being protected, and they are able to develop and express this knowing through the making and appreciation of symbolic forms.

A word of warning about dancing feelings and symbolized feeling. There is a propensity to link dance expression with emotion because real emotion is often expressed bodily. Children are frequently invited to do a dance about being sad, happy, or angry, but being sad and expressing sadness are not the same thing. Being sad is an attitude, it is a response to something that arouses feelings of sadness and might be more appropriately expressed somewhere alone rather than in a school dance lesson with thirty other children! Sadness is expressed in dance through the qualities of shape, time, movement, and relationships, and these are explored and formulated because they have some affinity with the nature of sadness, not because they are sad.

The ability to be expressive is dependent on a knowledge of the symbolic language, its structure and its vocabulary. To express an idea of a feeling in a foreign language obviously requires a knowledge of that language. Expression in dance is likewise dependent on knowing the language of dance and the availability of the physical and compositional skills. If children are to be expressive and able to formulate ideas in dance they must have the means of doing so.

This knowledge can be discovered, given and practised, or searched for. Children come to a dance lesson with a movement vocabulary of their own — after all they have been learning to move for a long time — but this knowledge is not necessarily available as dance knowledge, so that the dance lesson is often about becoming more aware of what is known. In a dance study about disintegration, the children will need to consider change of body and group shape, management of body weight, continuity, and some control of falling. Learning to fall might well be just a skills practice, learning to express disintegration as a group might require some investigation of objects in different stages of disintegration and the exploration of gestures experimenting with shapes that capture a breaking-up feeling. Exploration includes improvisation, observation, development, manipulation, and selection. The ability to select, to refine, and to put the movement ideas into some kind of logical order makes expression possible. Expression without this structure of the language is likely to be superficial and meaningless.

33

Ideas, feelings, sensation and experiences are given form through the dance activity. Formulation involves seeing connections and relationships and requires an ability to bring together related material with understanding. A dance about circles might include the consideration and exploration of rotation, cycles, cyclic motion, a never-ending sequence, waxing and waning, being divided, segments, enclosing, and excluding. A dance using a single figure might explore aloneness, the individual, the absence of others, freedom and the limitation of being alone, introspection, non-procreation. This process of formulating ideas through dance is conceptual, it brings together associated and related ideas in a context that makes understanding possible and necessary.

The formulated content of dance must be shareable and understandable to others. Its success as a communication depends on that form being possible although imagined, and reasonable although inventive. An art image deals with the subjective but its reference is shared reality and it is on the basis of the structure and order of reality that communication is made possible. If the image bears no resemblance to known reality, then that image is meaningless. Whatever the reference for making a dance, that reference as it exists is the basis for the created form. A dance about the ebb and flow of the sea must begin with an understanding of the sea's motion, a dance about lack of freedom must explore how a lack of freedom comes about and its effect on the way people behave and occupy space. When children make dance in school they are concerned not only with the nature of expression, they are concerned also with the nature of what is being expressed.

Dance Within the Curriculum

In this chapter I have outlined the time/space nature of dance, the bodily experience, and dance as a means of expression and communication. The validity of these as learning activities and the development of the understanding of dance as a symbolic form places dance firmly in the arts, but many school curricula include dance in the Physical Education programme, as does the national curriculum. This needs some explanation.

Dance was first established in British schools in PE for very good reasons, some of which still apply. Dance is bodily movement and physical skill, dancers require an open space and a good floor surface, clothes are often worn to facilitate movement which might mean a change of clothing. Planning and styles of teaching have to take into account the management of thirty or more moving bodies in free space, and the teacher's own active participation. Dance needs a gym or hall space as do games and gym, so that it seems reasonable to timetable dance in the same subject slot. Another factor is that Rudolph Laban's teaching and analysis of movement in education was introduced into school by physical educationalists and it was their enthusiasm that established dance as an educational subject in this country. Some PE teachers took on board many of Laban's theories about dance so that ideas about floor pattern, change of speed and body awareness, for example, appeared in gymnastics, even in some games activities, and dance was added to the PE programme.

PE emphasizes the physical nature of dance and the science of movement. The physical activity of games and gymnastics is objective and public; the structure and skill of games playing is functional; the run, jump, and throw of athletics is measurable, and the gymnast, however aesthetic, demonstrates physical skill. The attitude toward physical ability is about efficiency, prowess and competition. The attitude towards physical ability in dance is secondary, it is a means of expression, of communication, of ordering and forming subjective experience, there is no place for competition when the emphasis is on individuality. The style of teaching and the atmosphere in the learning space must reflect that subjectivity. If the children are to understand dance they must develop an appropriate attitude to the learning situations, they have to be in a situation where they can sense, feel, imagine, create and share, and feel sufficiently confident to share the private self with others. An artistic attitude is required. The teacher too has to present himself and the work appropriately which is a problem for the specialist PE teacher in secondary education who may have to teach a dance lesson between athletics and football. It requires less of a change of attitude to teach a dance lesson between music and drama.

This is also true of learning resources. Dance literature is fairly inadequate, but much that is written about visual art, music, sculpture and drama provides relevant reading. The fact that literature for dance is to be found on the art shelf is significant.

Dewey described the curriculum as 'a crystallization of human experience', but that experience is conveniently categorized into subjects to collect together methods, concepts and practices which enable us to manage and deal with the many different facets of experience. Attitudes, kinds of activities and kinds of thinking differ and must be selected according to the kind of knowledge children are engaged in. Even in the primary classroom integrated day there are changes of equipment, place, mood and clothing according to the nature of the activity. The contribution of these particular activities is reflected in particular goals or objectives which emphasize subject knowledge, whereas general aims express and reflect the whole nature of learning within and outside school. Valid implementation and interpretation of these aims is dependent on bringing the two together. The following examples show how:

(1) To learn how to make decisions according to personal and shared judgment.

Dance is about selecting a starting point, selecting movement vocabulary and method of working, identifying and clarifying the essential, deciding who to work with, making decisions about sound, techniques, and presentation; selecting and refining ideas appropriately; recognizing the abilities of the group.

(2) To learn how to accept the responsibility for making a choice or making a decision.

Dance will require sensitive social interaction, self-confidence, knowing when to lead or follow, being supportive, a commitment to others and to the work, ability to express and consider ideas in verbal and movement language, a tolerant and positive attitude, and involved and sustained interest to complete the project.

(3) To learn how to become informed and skilled in order to accept that responsibility.

Dance will make demands on the ability to notice, discover and investigate; use resources; acquire and practice performance skills and techniques; improvise and innovate; and understand composition.

(4) To notice and respond to the physical and sensed environment, to question it, to improve it, to protect it and to appreciate it.

Dance provides the opportunity to share, explore and consider ideas, feelings and experiences; to examine and interpret form; to order, emphasize and search for meaning in form; to formulate and express response to the environment in a communicable form; to create form; to become aware of the relationship between form and function; to become aware and develop an aesthetic appreciation of form.

(5) To learn about oneself, to recognize one's abilities and limitations, feelings and ideas.

Dance is about the subjective; the body is an instrument of expression and performance is about the presentation of the self. It is about reviewing one's personal contribution of physical and technical skills, imagination, creativity, and level of understanding. It is about making public ideas and feelings.

(6) To recognize and appreciate other feelings and ideas, experiences and viewpoints that may differ from ones own.

Dance is a social art form and involves the sharing of ideas and abilities. Appreciation of dance works and the work of other artists brings the children in contact with similar and contrasting interpretations and points of view.

Children engaged in the above activities learn a great deal about dance, but they are learning much more. Children go to school to learn — not to DO maths, or DO science, or DO dance. The nature of the activity facilitates and orders learning. What matters most is the teacher who understands learning experience as a whole and can select and interpret parts of that whole as worthwhile and appropriate content and activity. This chapter has set out the nature of dance activity to facilitate that understanding and place dance, as a way of learning, in and across the curriculum. Consider the following:

- Language: about the ability to formulate and communicate ideas and experiences.
  Through dance?
- Science: about awareness of the environment, developing a sense of responsibility about the environment, about investigation, interpretation and recording.
  Using dance?
- Maths: about change, the transformation of shape and the ability to understand the nature of change and structure.
  Using dance?
- Music: about rhythm and phrase.
  With dance?
- Physical education: the body as a means of expression.
  As dance?
- Social interaction:
  In dance?
- Art: about line and shape.
  Of dance?

3
Teaching Strategies and Planning

Introduction

Planning and teaching methods are often determined by objectives and aims. This book describes what dance is rather than what it is for. It is left to the teacher to select appropriate activities and dance ideas according to the children's needs and the learning context.

In the past dance has been a vehicle for many human activities, for worship, magic, celebration, sacred rites, theatre, and social behaviour. Out of these has grown the art of dance, a relatively new art form and a new curriculum subject, but one that retains evidence of its genetic origins. Witness the trance-like performance in pop dance and music, the ritual of gesture, and processions on religious or state occasions. Dance is a powerful medium, and is brought under control in the context of school and by the process of ordering the art of the dance form.

When children are engaged in an activity, their behaviour is disciplined by the medium of that activity. Children in a swimming pool cannot run in the water, lie down or jump in the deep end if they cannot swim — the medium itself controls their behaviour. When children work with clay, their ideas, sensations and feelings come under the influence of the way clay is. Similarly, children moving in a dance lesson are disciplined by the structure of making dance.

Children dancing are engaged in spatial temporality, in the physical movement of the body and in social interaction. Discipline comes from the control of gravity and energy, from ordering movement ideas, from sharing and creating form, and from the meaning in the form. Dance is essentially aesthetic in that it is about form, it is a language in that it is about meaning in form, it is an art in that it creates expressive form.

When teachers plan activities, or ask the children questions or steer an activity, they need to have some sense of purpose, to have something in mind that colours the what, the why and the how. It is all too easy to follow a plan without teasing out the deeper implications or to praise without understanding the real significance and potential of the activity. A group of children have completed a dance study. 'Good', you say, because the movements are precise and the children have worked well together. But what about the sequence itself? What have they discovered? Why in that order? What have the children 'said'? What follows? How should a second sequence be considered? Would that be logical? How do they know it is logical? They have started something ... what?

The teacher has to have a view of learning that goes further than the subject matter. An awareness of form in dance is also an awareness of form in our surroundings, in our social environment. Awareness carries with it responsibility, the responsibility of expressing ideas and feelings in dance is also about *having* ideas and feelings and consciously dealing with them. How we do that depends on our own long view of knowledge and our ability to use appropriate strategies for the children we teach. We have to find a way of involving the children so that the work matters, so that they experience the driving force of being interested, and the commitment of 'belonging'.

Finding the Way In

Getting the Children Involved

Who are the children? What interests them? What can they do? What do they know? What would they like to know? What should they know? How do they operate socially in the classroom? What is interesting about where they live? What do you, the teacher, find interesting? What is the relationship between teacher and children?

Starting with the children's interests is not dancing freely to their chosen records. It is about finding a lively interaction between the children, the teacher, and the subject matter. It is an interaction that invites contribution, that sparks off a new awareness, that questions what is known, that teaches something new and develops existing knowledge. To be interested is to accept the obligation of that interest, a group of children who want to present dance for a morning assembly must accept the responsibility of making that performance worthwhile and polished, a responsibility that has to be arrived at, not battled for.

Begin with where the children are, but recognize the difference between experiences that are relevant and available and those that belong to the child's private life or are as yet unformed in consciousness.

Possible starting points include the immediate and real experience provided by the school building: draw, measure, compare drain-pipes and roofs, feel the texture of bricks, weigh them and find out how much it costs to build a wall ... why not build a wall?

Focus on the self, on the body, how it works and what can go wrong with it, look at x-rays of bones, draw, measure, and take photographs of each other. Draw and make facial expressions and gestures, make and use masks and gloves or finger masks. Draw body shapes that are balancing, pointing, resting,

39

curled or extended. Persuade a parent or grandparent or headteacher to sit for a portrait.

Start with fun. Walk with paint to paint footprints; look at reflections in mirrors, spoons and puddles. Dance in different clothes or wellington boots. Use the weather to be blown in the wind, to feel cold hands, to collect rain, to fashion the snow. Do magic things like developing photographic prints or making silhouettes of each other with an OHP. Smuggle a chair into the classroom, arrange the classroom chairs as if the day is spent on a long-distance bus, use the gym mats as if they are magic carpets or the benches as part of the hold of a ship.

Awaken an awareness of form by collecting objects that are cherished, old, secret, rare, battered, decaying. Describe them, draw them, classify them. Instead of bombarding the children with visual display, copy the Japanese: give one article a place of prominence and give it special attention just for a day. Instead of swopping weekend news, talk about one common event or one special object.

Create interests by making the children and their classroom special. Have special visitors, special projects, special places for a book or 'thinking quietly' corner. Have an occasional special day, make special lunch or playtime arrangements, be occasionally very special yourself.

Finding the Significance

Dance is a metaphoric form distanced from reality; the distance makes subjectivity objective. The meaning in dance lies in its perceived qualities of form, not in the actual qualities of movement itself. A dance lesson in which body shapes are explored is also about the feel or look of the shapes and the reason and consequence of making a shape different.

Doing dance is about finding or recognizing the significance of the action and the idea. The significant moment in the parable of The Good Samaritan could be the moment of commitment, the moment at which the passing traveller makes some kind of contact with the injured man. The significance of that moment in the dance is stated in the focus of the eyes, in the posture and by the proximity of the body. Freeze that moment in the dance study to explore the meaning and possible alternatives.

Perceiving significance in relationship and form is facilitated by exploring real examples: the way something is attracted to another can begin with the observation of magnets and iron filings, with bubbles merging, with colours running together, with paying attention to the possible relationship between dropped pebbles, or by looking at the relationship between objects in pictures, between people in photographs.

Dance activity involves the children in different social relationships and social interaction. There is the social activity of working together, making decisions and talking about the work, but more peculiar in dance is the objective human relationship of two or more bodies creating body images together. When two bodies create an image of, say, lines crossing, or a body heap, bodies come into very close physical contact, the bodies are instrumental. The image may also represent a close emotional relationship and often does in classical ballet love duets. This close relationship and close physical contact, whilst being objective, includes the subjectivity of real relationships and real closeness. Although children's school dance is unlikely to include love duets, bodies do come into close physical contact. This kind of relationship requires much trust and an ability to explore objective physical contact. This can be encouraged and demonstrated in activities which explore physical relationships such as taking each other's weight, leading a blindfold partner, mirroring actions, 'making' sculptures, exploring group shape and group interaction. Reference to real physical images will help children to use themselves in this instrumental way: a broken relationship might be symbolized by a snapped twig leaving broken ends, or by clay being separated and rejoined, or water flowing back when parted. Opposition might be physically explored and experienced by pulling and pushing against a partner then repeating this without physical contact, so that the opposition is imagined.

Concrete images of form help to make the dance less abstract. Children can find movement ideas by referring to real images, a practice shared by all artists.

Change	Ice melting, paper burning, leaves wilting, ink in water, screwed paper unfolding, yeast growing, water evaporating, spaghetti cooking.
Dispersing and coming together	Smoke from a snuffed candle, a deflating balloon, iron filings drawn to a magnet, spilt peas, spilt water, children coming to school, people entering a railway station, blown litter, swept leaves, a vacuum cleaner.
Increase and decrease	Inflating a balloon, breathing, seeds growing, folding paper, the moon, tides, a bath filling, shadows in sunshine, a car approaching.
Shape	Shells, buildings, scaffolding, rocks, paint and blots, vegetables and fruit cut in half, prickles and thorns, concave mirrors, reflections, mouths and eyes in laughter, clouds, hands.
Movement	Smoke, balls rolling, water dripping, clouds forming, waves breaking, wind-blown grass, pistons and wheels, elastic, a tissue falling.

Knowledge of form is about observing form and experiencing form. This makes possible the recognition and manipulation of form.

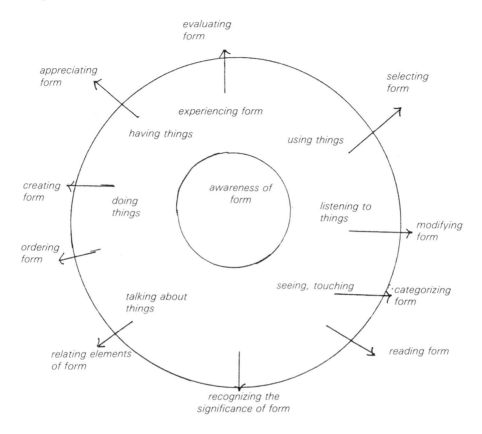

Understanding the Rules of the Medium

This is about knowing how dance works, what it is made of and how meanings are revealed in body movement. Some of this knowledge comes from the experience of others, from those who have danced in the past, those who dance professionally, and those who write about dance. We do not start experiences from scratch, as it were, but inherit knowledge, techniques, skills, principles, and behaviour, and these become rules for procedure.

There are two ways of using these rules in the dance lesson.

(1) Governed by rules
The children's work is controlled by the rules, they learn specific movements and patterns of movement and tested techniques for skilful body management. Composition is based on given form and meanings are expressed according to given codes so that a product of some sort is assured.

The advantages of rule-based work: the children use tangible and concrete methods, a high level of skill usually means a high level of achievement, those who fail do so because they have not learnt the rules, the teacher is usually the judge. The teacher works according to the prescribed structure which is comforting and which forecasts the outcome, providing a norm for assessment.

The disadvantages: the rules are prescriptive and success is rated according to how well rules are kept. Knowledge becomes divisive so that participants succeed or fail. The rules are given by others living in another place or at another time. Those who challenge the rules or discover new rules are unaccepted.

(2) Rules discovered

The children use rules or arrive at them; rules enable. Past works and knowledge are investigated to support the children's own work. Ways of working are negotiated, children and teacher work together and accept the responsibility for what has been negotiated.

Advantages: interest in the work is likely because the learning arises out of the children's own experience and ideas. This means that they, and their work, matter. The children can be challenged and demands made of them through their own contribution, and this contribution becomes necessary. As the work comes into being the maker is given responsibility, the dance begins to matter, and a commitment is set in motion.

Disadvantages: discovering rules is a risky business, the rule book is replaced by negotiation through which the children discover their own need of existing rules or find their own. Confidence in the self and in the children is required along with a sound understanding of the material and the subject matter; this could be different for each child or group of children.

Whatever brand of teaching is used, the teacher must have a working knowledge of the rules, the techniques, and the procedures in order to give the work any substance and recognizable achievement. Some information is essential whether it features as a prescription or as something to be discovered.

Given rules

Rules		*Children*
govern the use of movement structure the composition control skill	that govern	work according to rules use established skills work towards a specific product fail or succeed

Discovered rules

Rules		*Children*
describes the dance: refers to acquired rules and supports work	that enable	discover rules negotiate the rules investigate existing rules failure and success is part of the process, and is shared.

(source: Bruner, 1986)

Enabling guidelines

Rudolph Laban's analyses of movement: dance is ACTION performed by the BODY in SPACE and TIME; significance is given by the spatial and temporal organization, by the DYNAMIC qualities and the RELATIONSHIPS that occur.

Examples would be:

(1) Stepping ... foot to foot ... forwards ... in a repeated metric duple rhythm ... with broken continuity

or

(2) Stepping ... bottom to tummy to knee ... rotating, with extension and contraction ... very slowly ... smooth with decreasing force. Relationships ... opposition to the floor, moving away from the floor, encircling and closing in.

(3) Hovering ... with the whole body ... at a high level ... alternating still and moving phrases. Relationship ... watching, mirroring, dominating.

This analysis helps to build a varied vocabulary and stimulates invention. Running, for example, can be fast, slowing down, in circles, with a partner, backwards, with large steps, accentuated on every third step, as if fatigued or escaping.

Rules for composition can be found in rules for music composition. Examples are: theme and variation, ABA, rondo, a suite, building to a climax, question and answer, a round or fugue.

Performance rules might include rules about skill and behaviour: clarity, projection, attention to appearance such as not wearing jewelry, not mixing dance styles, always using music, acceptable subject matter and body display.

Appreciation rules about what is a successful dance work might show harmony, balance, invention, proportion, pace, accuracy, alignment, strength and flexibility, grace, beauty, vitality, surprise, relevance.

Dance in school rules — such as: dance is only done in the hall, children must change their clothes, the teacher must follow the radio programme, children must be quiet, dance must be supervised, children must work together. Rules are sometimes necessary and sometimes are quite inappropriate but become established through thoughtless acceptance.

Developing the Child, Developing the Work

The child learns by interacting with others, by responding to the demands of the activity, by handling materials and thinking appropriately. The teacher must recognize the teaching potential of an activity and facilitate or extend learning by using what that activity is: its content, skills, techniques, information and attitude. The criteria lie in the ultimate realization of the activity, thus the criteria for a science project is the way a scientist works, the 5-year-old pouring water is an embryo scientist, the 7-year-old making dance is an embryo choreographer. Although the child is not necessarily on the way to becoming a scientist or choreographer, the child is an embryo adult and by answering the kind of problems a dancer or scientist or any other specialist has to answer, the child is using tried and untried ways of dealing with the external world.

Dance-making engages the child in stages of responding, doing, creating, selecting, refining, and presenting. The following example shows how an infant class might begin by sensing and then interpreting their sensed experience in different media.

Sensing and Response

The children watch an apple being peeled, they see and touch the peel, they become interested and involved.

Actively Responding

The children notice the shape of the peel as it winds and unwinds. They reconstruct the shape of the peel and compare it to the original apple shape. The children make a body shape like that of the peel, and more to explore ways of winding and unwinding.

45

Mary Lowden

Development and Awareness

The children explore other movements that unwind, they dance unwinding shapes as if willingly and then against opposition. They explore continuity by moving bit by bit with increasing speed. In twos, they explore the relationship between the outside and the inside, they 'unpeel' as a group and recall folk dance patterns from a previous lesson.

Creating

The children make three phrases of movement based on the unwinding and winding idea. They vary the length of the phrases, add accents and travel. They look at other shapes that can be peeled, torn, moulded, thrown, untwisted; and explore other interpretations and ways of moving.

Selection

The children drop unwound string onto a pasted board.

They use these shapes as a dance score manipulating the string patterns and chosen movements. They print the string shapes on top of each other to make and find patterns for dance.

In twos they use the idea of this pattern to create a dance.

Development

The teacher adds tasks which direct or suggest further ideas. Children might exaggerate the interweaving, exploit any chance relationships, or develop the lead and follow the idea. Tasks must be supportive yet challenging. Unnecessary tasks inhibit, irritate and even kill off any imagination.

The children can play with the idea by moving into a different environment: the corridor, outside, the swimming pool.

Presentation and Sharing

The work is shared and discussed. The children look at similar ideas in another art form: in sculpture, poetry, drawing. They add information from other curriculum subjects and are able to comment on other unwinding shapes, found in food, and protective covering.

Developing this idea in another way

Apple ... string ... design ... print-making.
Apple ... string ... dance ... ritual ... pattern.
Apple ... string ... movement ... song ... words ... poetry.
Apple ... movement ... rhythm ... percussion ... time values ... numeracy.
Apple ... clay ... structure.
Apple ... pattern ... stepping ... notation ... using the turtle ... logo.

Other Starting Points

Rubbings of wire mesh, drain covers, tyre marks, stepping in time to a song, selecting sections of scribble drawings, moving in and out of objects, moving in a confined space such as a cornflakes box, work actions using rolled newspaper as a tool, playing with dough or elastic, making sculpture with wire, paper, clay, or plaster.

Dealing with Problems

Different Expectations

The parent: Dance is as they remember in their own primary school, when they were asked to be a butterfly or a daffodil, and it had little educational value.

47

Answer: Present some successful dance work for a parents' evening. Include information and guidelines for watching. Show the thinking and planning that the children are engaged in, including the way ideas developed to reach presentation level. The dance work might be examples of learning rather than a performance. Involve the parents in 'mini' movement tasks which they do or think about later. Include some classwork in a parents' evening so that they can see their children working with others. Have something to show for the term's work such as follow-up writing, drawing or video, or the children's plans for their dance. It is important that parent and school visitors do not base their impression of the school solely on bookwork.

★ ★ ★ ★

The headteacher: Dance is performance, excellent for Christmas, morning assembly or Friday afternoons but not a lot to do with academic study.

Answer: S/he is right, but what does this performance entail? Show and explain how movement work is a way of learning and is sometimes the most appropriate way. Plan a performance that grows out of classwork and show how the dance contributes to the development of understanding in other subject areas.

★ ★ ★ ★

The staff: Teaching dance is for the expert or the energetic, it is easier to do country dance, use the radio programme, or get someone else to do it.

Answer: Talk to the staff, help them with planning, share ideas and difficulties. Try some team teaching sharing different starting points and strategies, such as movement and music, shape in movement and maths, design in clay and dance, poetry and movement. Don't go on about dance being the answer to everything and how your children are good at it! Run some staff workshops.

If the radio programme is a tradition, draw attention to the introductory and follow-up work booklet. Use the radio programme yourself as a starter, develop and share ideas.

★ ★ ★ ★

The children: Dance is what people do at discos or on *Top of the Pops*.

Answer: Start here. Use these ideas but extend the material, so that a bit of disco progresses, perhaps fit a different rhythm or context.

★ ★ ★ ★

The children: Dance is playing about in the hall, you can do what you like ... shout, slide, bump into others, chat, roll on the mats. It's silly.

Answer: Don't call it dance, don't change clothing. Use the hall time to draw a large map, to take still photographs, to test the pulse rate during rest and exercise, to imagine or remember an obstacle course when blindfolded. Combine activities so that some children draw, write, record sound, while others move. Plan some movement puzzles such as getting off the floor in six moves, exactly repeating a partner's action, crossing the space without using the feet. Prepare ground work in the classroom before working in the hall.

★ ★ ★ ★

Other Problems

Lack of space: There is no space to dance in.

Answer: Adapt the classroom. Do movement that takes up little space such as using hands only, or puppets, or mobile sculpture. Run a dance club at lunch time, negotiate for a hall time, exploit any opportunity such as when the head needs something for assembly or an open evening or a festival.

Avoid taking dance lessons outside — the space is not conducive to concentration or privacy.

★ ★ ★ ★

Lack of support: There is little support from other staff.

Answer: Don't be too energetic or enthusiastic. Do your own thing quietly and well. If it works your children will be your best ambassadors. Share some of the work as part of a project and emphasize the opportunity for learning rather than for performance. Don't dance about in the staffroom — you have to have an amazing charisma or insensitivity to get away with jazzy clothes and an evident body however trim it might be!

★ ★ ★ ★

Grasshoppers: These are children with abundant and uncontrollable energy.

Answer: Channel the energy, give it a frame, contrast energy with stillness, play games that encourage concentration, play games about making statues, move close to the floor as if the ceiling was a metre high, travel getting slower and slower, respond to 'special' signals. Change the approach by not changing clothes, by sitting and listening. Use a small space, draw and then dance the drawing, watch and discuss examples of movement, use the gym mats as the only place where movement *can* happen, postpone the dance work until the class are ready for this activity.

★ ★ ★ ★

Dormice: Children who find the movement and the space very threatening.

Answer: Offer an alternative activity that contributes to the dance work. Give time for children to adjust to and become familiar with this way of working. Do activities that take the focus away from the self, avoid any task that isolates individual differences, provide a home base such as a chair, a mat or a sheet or paper. Start the work in the security of the classroom, then take it into the hall.

★ ★ ★ ★

Anyone: Dance is embarrassing

Answer: Of course it is, you are asking people to explore and reveal some of their inner privacy in a very public situation, using bodies to do so. Understand that not everyone is able or prepared to use the body as a means of shared expression and that bodily functions are normally associated with privacy, they are rude, uncontrollable and subversive. The dance activity must demonstrate that the use of the body in dance is a product of will, that it is an instrument of thought, of forming ideas, and that there is a language syntax, however loose, that is identifiable. Base the movement on gestures that are used and read every day, on how we manage gravity, on the way the body occupies space, and on the way shapes and actions set up recognizable relationships.

★ ★ ★ ★

Resources: Dance is a comparatively new subject, there are very few books.

Answer: Many art books are very relevant, in particular books about visual art, three-dimensional art, and art education. On the plus side, dance is an inexpensive subject. It requires space and a good floor surface. Bodies, objects for reference and percussive sound can come for free. Sophisticated video and audio equipment is an exciting addition, but not essential.

The Roles of the Teacher

The teacher's role is created in answer to the interaction between the teacher's personal qualities and the circumstances of teaching. The role of the teacher is no more predetermined than the role of individuals in contemporary society, and each lesson will use a range of strategies and presentations which should be considered during the preparation.

Although this interaction is intuitive it is easy to fall into a mode of teaching which becomes habitual and which serves any class lesson and any group of children, a habit which might be cultivated by a national curriculum when taught to the same age group for several years. Consideration of appropriate and possible roles also makes conscious a teacher's beliefs and principles, and reflects the teacher's view of the job which is ...?

(1)   The teacher is knowledgeable and passes on what he knows. The teacher informs, instructs, directs and decides.
(2)   The teacher learns and passes on subject material. Subjects are bodies of knowledge, each having particular information, skills, techniques, kinds of thinking, and ways of working.
(3)   The teacher plans and organizes activities so that the children come to know subjects, some of which the teacher learns with the children.
(4)   The teacher sets up activities and provides information based on the children's needs and interests.
(5)   The teacher feeds in skills, techniques and information enabling the children to develop their skills and ideas according to a particular objective.

A teacher combines a variety of roles at any one time. Consider:

●   A teacher is a friend and helper who supports, suggests, listens, encourages, participates, and persuades.
●   A teacher is a controller who interferes when necessary, redirects, rechannels, makes decisions, plans and assesses, organizes, interprets the school or national programme, follows and interprets a syllabus.
●   A teacher is a consultant who collects and suggests resources, coaches skills, observes and advises, sets up activities that teach, organizes visits and visitors, suggests and arbitrates.
●   A teacher is a thinker who questions and challenges ideas, promotes critical appraisal, and asks for information.

The Teacher as a Motivator

This is about making learning as relevant and as real as possible. Search for objects, events and experiences that will lead the children into more knowing. Start from what is on hand, show the children that knowing is exciting, and is a revelation about the world and about oneself.

This means being an interesting person, looking interesting and having exciting experiences yourself. Do something to charge up the batteries, a night out might sometimes be time better spent than lesson planning! Be interested in the subject matter whether it is 'yours' or not, become informed, talk about it to others and do some of the activities.

Find your own stimulus for wanting to know. Recognize exciting ideas in the environment. Use the school and the playground, and invent uses for the classroom. Can the furniture be moved to change the focus or the nature of an activity? The classroom is perhaps a space planet, a laboratory, a field centre, a theatre, a medieval cloister.

What does the environment offer? Make a list: new buildings and scaffolding, poor architecture, bridges, roofs, chimneys, walls, drains, gutters, a view from the window, plants, walkways across grass, fences, people, grandparents with memories, workmen with jobs. Can any items be measured, talked about, costed, investigated as ideas for dance?.

Look at litter, look at the shape of crumpled crisp packets or collapsed tins, look at litter in the wrong place, litter being scattered by people, by the wind, litter recycled.

Collect, draw and group objects according to their shape, size, appeal, whether they seem ugly, harmonious, disturbing or pleasing. Group body movements and body shapes in similar categories.

Look at roofs, look at the relationship between the horizontal, vertical, and diagonal lines, look at angles of pitch, at gables and triangles, look at group shapes and the effect of distance and viewpoint. Look at slates and hand-made clay tiles. Are they smooth, regular, flat, thin, brittle, compressed, rigid? Explore these qualities in movement.

Consider the function of a roof, use the way water runs off into gutters and drains, create a class dance about collecting, funnelling, and getting rid of water.

Look at windows, at letting in light, look at the direction and pathway of light, the angles and shape of light as it falls on the floor or up the wall, look at the changing shape and place of shadows and the difference between light and darkness. In twos, be a shadow for a partner, dance the coming of light, contrast movements, words, sounds and group formations to compare the world of darkness and the world of sunlight. Dance the transition from one to the other.

The Teacher as a Negotiator

Make being in your classroom safe and exciting, generate a sense of ownership and pride. Have Friday sharings with another class to show work or bring ideas together. Share the running of the classroom, negotiate the placing of furniture, delegate as much as possible so that the room belongs to the children, and include the caretaker in the discussions!

Make knowledge something that is discovered together, ask the children for help and information, brainstorm together to find ways of starting or developing a project. Let the children feel that the ideas are theirs so that organization and the reward of achievement is shared.

Plan your questions and comments. Questioning is about negotiating. A question should invite children to contribute, not to guess what is in the teacher's mind ... children are very astute when it comes to picking up clues from a question! what is a question for? To find out? To challenge? To share information? To get the child to question himself?

Negotiation depends on trust and enthusiasm by which the teacher can influence the children instead of imposing on them, and these are qualities that must be sincere. If there is no trust the teacher must find ways of establishing trust; if there is no enthusiasm, it must be generated.

Encourage negotiation amongst the children: let them delegate, appoint leaders, share skills, be resources for each other, sort out team responsibilities, edit and appraise each other's work, so taking on a variety of roles themselves.

The Teacher as Enabler

Approach new knowledge from existing knowledge. Plan stages of learning so that the children are equipped to begin each stage.

Overcome difficulties by finding alternatives:

- If a child lacks the necessary balancing skills for a dance study, change the stance, provide a support, or coach balance
- If a child finds it difficult to work with others, give very clear tasks for working in twos, let the child work alone until there is something ready to be shared, let the child work with a chosen companion, or practice the idea with the teacher first
- If a child finds dance very threatening, provide alternative contributions such as working with the video camera, making a sound accompaniment, drawing or writing about other children's movement, working in another way that can be incorporated
- If a child lacks confidence and has few ideas, borrow ideas from others, work with those who are confident in a sharing task
- If a child has difficulty explaining ideas, share discussion, give time and opportunity to practise explaining, draw ideas, try spoken ideas on an audio tape, and written ideas on a word processor
- If a child has no suitable clothing, use what he has, or provide an alternative.

Enable yourself as a teacher; do activities that work, build up a repertoire, and gradually introduce more risky ideas as you become confident. Plan well but include alternatives, avoid threatening situations and find ways to manage difficulties; talk about your work with other teachers.

Think of knowledge and teaching techniques as resources. When planning a project, list available resources, including the children's; list skills, techniques and information that are necessary but not ready or available; teach, discover, explore, investigate, and practise that which is required. Identify the possible requirements and make a 'shopping list'.

Mary Lowden

In a project about the sea the list might read as follows: Is the sea an available resource? If the answer is 'no', is there any point in thinking about the sea? If the answer is 'yes', what do the children already know about the sea and what skills do they have?

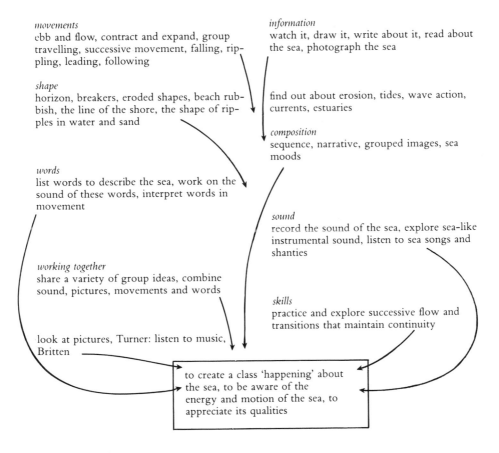

movements
ebb and flow, contract and expand, group travelling, successive movement, falling, rippling, leading, following

information
watch it, draw it, write about it, read about the sea, photograph the sea

shape
horizon, breakers, eroded shapes, beach rubbish, the line of the shore, the shape of ripples in water and sand

find out about erosion, tides, wave action, currents, estuaries

composition
sequence, narrative, grouped images, sea moods

words
list words to describe the sea, work on the sound of these words, interpret words in movement

sound
record the sound of the sea, explore sea-like instrumental sound, listen to sea songs and shanties

working together
share a variety of group ideas, combine sound, pictures, movements and words

skills
practice and explore successive flow and transitions that maintain continuity

look at pictures, Turner: listen to music, Britten

to create a class 'happening' about the sea, to be aware of the energy and motion of the sea, to appreciate its qualities

Evaluation

Question the validity of the activities. What was learnt and how? What have the children learnt for themselves and about themselves? What has been learnt about movement, the sea, composition, performance, social interaction, shape and motion? How can this be interpreted, applied, developed?

The Teacher as Controller

Control is related to power. The teacher's power is balanced by the power of the children; the teacher's ability to motivate, negotiate and enable is dependant upon this balance of power, a balance that is about mutual trust and respect.

The teacher's power is founded on a variety of factors: the position of one adult amongst many; knowledge and skills that appear superior; apparent freedom of choice compared to restricted behaviour; a self-chosen occupation compared to a required occupation; professional status supported by the authority of government, law and church; the power of literacy, of the book and the pen.

There are other factors that are discretionary: the power of competition; of classroom organization; rows of desks; seating according to some kind of hierarchy; the place of the teacher's desk; forms of address.

The Power of the Children

Their power lies in the fact that the teacher's sense of success is dependent on the children's achievement. Achievement depends on interest and interaction between teacher and children, and effective interaction depends on communication, on how well the teacher has access to who the children really are, and children can deny this access. The children can have a poor profile of 'teacher' that is supported by their parents' memories of school, and by media fact and fiction. The children can obstruct whatever good intentions the teacher might have by being disinterested, disruptive, hostile, passive and, of course, absent!

The dance lesson has dispensed with many of the instruments of teacher power — no desks, no books, no competition, few academic rules, few examinations. The teacher has to negotiate lines of communication that are based on mutual respect and trust. In this task the teacher is supported by the nature of the activity. The lesson accommodates close participation without loss of teacher status. In a dance lesson the teacher can sit on the floor, wear leisure clothing much the same as the children are wearing, and make physical contact with the children — hold hands, support bodies, be supported, sing, dance, play music.

This state of affairs also gives scope for uncooperative behaviour — the hall space, the physical activity, the leaving behind of desks and books, all make some alternative kind of control necessary.

Controlling the Dance Lesson

Getting ready. Is changing clothes necessary? If so, how long does it take? Often more time than the lesson! Teach skills like doing up laces and zips, encourage the children to help each other, use an egg timer to measure getting ready time, make undressing a part of the lesson. Maybe the children can take off their shoes to reveal magic feet that walk in special places!

Moving to the hall: Do the children charge down the corridor and disturb others? Start the lesson in the classroom, record the sound and measure the time of the 'journey', negotiate a system, make a game in which the children are smugglers or naturalists. Perhaps a corridor is a minefield or a tunnel under a magic castle.

Using the hall space: Are the children ready for this space? If the space is too big, section off a portion; if too cold, keep on warm clothing; if threatening, try an idea in the classroom first. Have controlling devices, practise going and stopping, have signals for stillness and learn them as a game, if it works keep to the routine. Have controlling objects such as a chair as a home base ... or a sheet of newspaper ... or a gym mat on which to show work. Plan controlling tasks such as playing statues, balancing, having half the class move while the others are still, alternating energetic activity with sudden changes to stillness and silence. Direct a variety of simple activities and keep up the pace without waiting for the dawdlers or inattenders. Use catchy music and create a simple sequence to go with it: lie, sit, stand, lie. Have a long list of fun things to do and note the ideas that work, repeat these ideas in several lessons gradually increasing the need to concentrate by increasing the level of skill.

Inappropriate class behaviour probably means that the class are not yet ready for the activity or that the work is inappropriate. Take note of 'high' moments of achievement and cooperation and exploit them. If the lesson is too long, cut it; if too difficult, make it easier; if boring, make it exciting, but only until the children understand the nature of the work, then challenge their skills and their ability to concentrate and work out ideas through chore stages, encourage attention even if the work is difficult. Never complain or nag.

Lack of concentration: Make success evident at each stage of the activity, use tangible examples, use yourself as the focus for 'copy me' or 'creep past me' or 'move when I am still'.

Noise: Speak quietly, practise listening, alternate noisy explosive movements with stillness, make a sound recording with the children and use it as a sound accompaniment, use quiet music. If the children talk too much, give them something to talk about in a context that controls the volume, alternate movement and talk with remaining still and silence, have noisy and quiet places to move in.

Teacher participation: Move with the children but do not demonstrate if they always copy your ideas; explain and coach as the children move so that they do not break continuity; use the voice as accompaniment; whisper, shout, speak with the rhythm, vary the speed, pitch and mood of the voice. Try being in role ... a magician who needs help with a spell ... a witch who is being secretly followed ... a scientist taking photographs of strange shapes ... an angry god who makes volcanos and earthquakes ... a wind that blows 'litter children'. Comment on the children's work positively even if this means turning a partial blind eye to the uninvolved — a word of praise elsewhere often encourages the inattentive. Encourage tryers and challenge the able. Have something more to say than 'good'. Why is it good? Does the work answer the task? How could it be developed? Use short movement sequences to emphasize the need for a controlled start and finish and the need to wait and watch quietly while others finish. Show your own respect for work by giving it your full attention.

Allow time to bring the lesson to a finish, try not to leave work unrecognized and unfinished, and do not expect children to remember work from one week to the next — if this is necessary keep an accurate record. Be consistent about behaviour going back to the classroom, recap work in the classroom and display related images, ideas and comments to demonstrate the validity of the work, do not leave it 'behind' in the hall.

Rationale

Going on a journey can be an exciting adventure and even a spontaneous decision but is almost impossible to undertake without some sense of direction. Teaching and being involved in learning activities is much like a journey, and although the actual destination may be unfamiliar or a surprise there must be some kind of reasoned driving force to make anything notable and worthwhile happen at all.

The 'destination' in education has many labels: objectives, aims, what the children will get out of the work, what the teacher hopes the children will achieve, what the children should be able to do or know as a result of the activity. Rationale or reasons for the activity also vary according to institutional or personal notions of what education is for anyway. Reasons may focus on a particular viewpoint according to the state of society, current thinking, politics and finance, the subject matter, the needs of the children, and the local environment.

Your own point of view or that of the school may represent a particular belief or vision. It is vital that both school staff as a whole and the individual teacher are aware of these beliefs and can review their thinking according to changes in policy and understanding. Teaching is not something to be learnt and repeated, it is an ever challenging and changing activity — the more successful the teaching the more the requirement to know more and use that knowledge.

The following sample of objectives represent different views which may reflect or question your own.

(1) The child is a potential adult member of society. Education must equip the individual to make reasoned judgments and decisions, and to contribute positively to that society.

(2) The child as a developing individual in a shared environment must be

      able to contribute, innovate, appreciate, respect, and share respon
      sibility for that environment.

(3)   The child as an inheritor of human endeavour and inspiration must
      reach appropriate levels of knowing and communication.

(4)   The child has certain needs, qualities and abilities that must be
      developed and catered for.

(5)   Activities and subjects have particular modes of practice and thought
      that are the basis of knowing.

(6)   A learning activity has value in its own right. Principles of procedure
      are more significant than objectives.

(7)   Knowledge should be based on the child's unique way of thinking
      and learning.

These objectives are long-term. Implementation and achievement are not confined to the years or place of schooling, but objectives have to be translated into activities that children and teachers actually do, into the schemes and lessons that are the building blocks. It is often difficult to keep goals in mind but constant reference to and revision of objectives will steer lesson preparation, influence teaching strategies and focus appraisal. However clear the goals and however well-planned the lessons, the clearest and most crucial directive comes from the children. Teaching is a dialogue and the materials we use, including the teachers and children, are dynamic. We might spark off something of value that we could not have foreseen, or labour a point the children have long since assimilated; we can awaken enlightenment and curiosity beyond our own experience and knowledge, or stifle a precious talent. One day is not like another, neither is one child or one class or one idea. We as teachers are not as we were last year, neither is the weather, or the environment or the classroom ethos, nor for that matter is national educational policy. We need sufficient knowledge and foresight to have a sense of direction and conviction, and sufficient awareness and open-mindedness to actively respond. Teaching is a creative occupation, and we have to make something with the materials of our vocation.

    Bearing in mind long-term rationale, ask yourself what you and the children are actually going to do, and distinguish between what you teach and what they learn — they are not necessarily synonymous; you may be preparing the children to control the use of space, they may be learning how to be bossed about!

    Break down the rationale into manageable stages, each being a foundation for the next, so that the children work effectively and manipulate skills and understanding accordingly. Remember that learning is not confined to subject activities; build on what the children learnt 'yesterday' rather than what they learnt in number work.

    In the following example, the objective (2, above) is broken down into the exploration and interpretation of form in the environment. The immediate environment offers scaffolding on a building site. The scaffolding is an example of functional ordering, and illustrates the relationship between vertical and horizontal lines. Children investigate the visual image and the way lines order the space. They look at the joints, and the effect of viewing the structure from different places. The children explore structural lines in space using body movement, they consider the relationship between lines, and lines that cross or join. Children make a group dance structure, they kinesthetically sense the relationship between up and down lines and across lines. Children find ways of moving into and out of the structure, they perform transitional movements that emphasize the quality of relationship within the structure. Children draw and describe other group studies, they compare the experiences of performance and spectator.

The experience of this activity will differ for each child. One might be more excited by the field work, another by drawing, another by the mathematical interpretation. The whole class activity might include experiences which remain private, and include noticing, appreciating, developing a body skill, being accepted in a group, having an idea that is valued, being informed, creating, enjoying movement, being rejected, being unskilled, being able to talk about the work at home. Whatever the activity, the teacher must try to 'get underneath' the essential content and the children's way in, so that the activity and the motivation develop ideas and abilities.

Appraisal of such an activity must again refer to the rationale so that the activity and the rationale are reassessed in the light of the children's response and possible development, in and beyond the particular activity. To complete the analogy, the traveller, having made the journey, considers the rewards and disappointments, and plans the next.

Planning the Programme

Introduction

If dance work in school is to have any value it must generate sufficient interest and challenge to involve the children in a worthwhile commitment. The work must be appropriate and achievement recognizable and accountable. It is obvious that there must be a curriculum plan; what is not obvious in many schools is that such a plan exists!

The curriculum syllabus brings together the way children are developing and learning and the way the subject matter develops. The subject is a vehicle for learning as well as something to learn. The development of knowledge and the way a child learns and develops is as a spiral, in which skills and understanding are continually revisited, appraised and built upon. This contrasts with curriculum plans that are usually written as stages of linear progression and planned according to the timetable and chronological academic years. Although we as teachers implement the curriculum along a period of time we must understand it as building upwards and outwards.

The following movement content shows progression according to the developmental stages of children. The material is only a guide since we are dealing with many children and therefore many kinds of development. However unrealistic this may be, we have to have a plan of some kind if children are to do progressively developing work. A lack of planning explains why so many lessons are the same whether a child is 5-years-old or 10.

The introductory work for the youngest children is basic and necessary for any age group being introduced to dance, it is the presentation that differs. Just as children learn by building on what they know, so the dance lesson recaps and reinforces what is known, it is because the children learnt about body weight management last term that they learn about it again, they will use that knowing in another way, in a more challenging or complex way. Learning is mostly about being aware of what is known, and the spiral of knowing is extended through awareness, by application and with information.

Nursery and Reception Age Group

Approach: The children's thinking is closely identified with body movement. Response to the environment is immediate and intuitive and is often more accurate in its perception than is realized, less so when the children have acquired a more sophisticated management of verbal language. Young children depend on picking up the right clues in adult body behaviour and are quick to respond to body language.

Body management: The quality and shape of movement is felt as a body activity. The floor is not far away and is accepted as part of the body environment so that rolling and tumbling is as much part of the normal vocabulary as walking and standing.

Making dance: Going and stopping, being fast and slow, making pathways and shapes — these activities are part of everyday behaviour; there is little difference between dancing and normal activity. The children actively explore changing levels, different textures and places as a natural response to where they are.

Significance: The children can understand contrast and change, they can compare high and low, fast and slow, movement and stillness.

Social: The children behave individually but in a shared space. They can work alongside each other and notice each other.

5 to 6 Years

Approach: Thinking is closely identified with physical activity and sensory experience. Children are able to respond with some sense of order and can distinguish between a dance action and everyday movement. They can understand the notion of the start and finish of movement duration, and can begin to reflect on, recall and label their movement.

Body awareness: Children begin to control body management, they can control and select parts of the body that move, support weight, and lead a movement. Children can play with floor contact, identify place, and combine change of body shape with changes of place and speed.

Making dance: Children can begin to select and make decisions about duration, direction, place and speed. They can understand contraction and extension in body shape and action, they can use words to describe simple dynamic qualities and respond to verbal tasks such as being jagged, continuous, twisted, opposite.

Significance: Children begin to understand and use images as representations and interpretations of experience. They can see connections between images of sound, sight, words and bodily movement. Children actively explore movement qualities in objects and action.

Social: Children are able to describe each other's movements, they can adapt space to accommodate others, they can take turns in a sequence and contribute individual ideas to classwork.

6 Years

Approach: Children can recognize, label, compare, and integrate variations. They can consider some movement ideas without necessarily moving and begin to have an objective view of physical activity.

Body awareness: Children can interpret shape with variations of speed, force, and action. They have a notion of appropriate selecting and ordering. They can achieve finely balanced body weight management and rapid changes of shape and placing. They can begin to polish and recall movement phrases.

Making dance. Children understand the effect of movement on space in simple actions; they have a notion of horizontality and verticality and can manipulate transitions and variations between the two dimensions. They are beginning to understand the relationship between distance and speed. They can follow a simple sound accompaniment and have a sense of dance performance.

Figure 6   Children begin to control and select parts of the body that move and support weight.

Significance: Children have a notion of affinity between simple shapes, actions, and dynamic qualities, and begin to reject or modify material accordingly.

Social: Children are able to lead and follow in a small group, they can choose who to work with or choose to work alone. They can help and accept help from others.

7 Years

Approach: Children can observe, recognize and consider qualities and properties. They have a notion of logical grouping and readily extend understanding by taking in new and novel experiences.

Body awareness: Children have a range of well-managed actions, they can manipulate actions according to given or self-selected tasks, they can pick up movements by watching others and repeat a short sequence fluently. They can describe and explain the sequence to others.

Making dance: The child is aware of his own body space as distinct from the general space, he can recognize spatial progression as an extension of spatial mass. Children can shape a sequence in space and time, they can use appropriate language and notation symbols.

Significance: The child understands the simple ordering of sequence including increase and decrease, gradual transition, change, and the forming of shape in time.

Social: The child begins to adapt movement ideas to small group compositions and explorations, and will try out ideas even if they are unformed.

7 to 8 Years

Approach: Children are aware of differences, they are able to consider variations of a single qualitative factor, and can see the relationship between two-dimensional and three-dimensional space and shape.

Body awareness: Children understand the body as an instrument of performance and expression, they can understand the need for good posture, control and management of energy and the need for skill acquisition.

Making dance Children have a notion of how three-dimensional space operates in the environment. They can recognize the finer variations of quality

63

in changes of speed, force and shape, they can phrase movements and place accents within a phrase. They are able to solve simple tasks within small group studies, they can use symbols or a written description as a starting point for creating dance.

Significance: Children are beginning to recognize factors that might determine changes in the quality of movement, and appreciate the significance of these qualities.

Social: Children's contribution to group work includes critical evaluation, selection, rejection, and manipulation of movement ideas.

8 Years

Approach: Children are able to consider cohesive and logical grouping, they can order, select and perform different qualities of movement, and justify the selection.

Body management: Children can critically appraise management of the body, they are aware of their strengths and limitations and can manipulate or acquire skills purposefully. They can learn another's sequence and teach their own.

Making dance: Children can use three-dimensional shape, volume and progression with relevant changes of speed, force, and pathway. They can perform subtle and obvious changes in shape, action, and dynamics. They can order movement ideas in a simple compositional form such as ABA or ABACADA.

Significance: Children can recognize, create and interpret relationship.

Social: Children can accept the responsibility for developing their own simple movement tasks. They can contribute to group work in differing roles.

8 to 9 Years

Approach: Children are prepared to manipulate material and entertain new ideas, they are willing to take risks, are adventurous and able to accept mistakes or failures as part of the process.

Body management: There is continued development of skills in relation to the development of ideas and movement exploration.

Making dance: Children can create, perform and evaluate simple movement compositions in small groups. They are able to select and investigate their own starting points and find their own motivation. They will improvise and try out ideas.

Social: Children have a working notion of group cooperation; they can accept and accommodate differing abilities.

9 Years

Approach: Children can manipulate concrete movement ideas. Manipulation leads to a discovery of meaning and therefore choice of movement qualities and actions. Children are beginning to explore dramatic, lyrical, comic, and formal dance styles. They are beginning to explore meaning in found objects and in improvised movement. They are beginning to identify what they discover and are able to share their discoveries.

Body management: Movement tasks make greater demands on the children's skills and sensitivity. They are beginning to try out skills and body movements, and improvisation leads to the discovery and exploration of new and unfamiliar material.

Making dance: Children explore feeling and expression in relation to various movement qualities and experiences. They are willing to improvise and then reflect as a way of discovering and interpreting ideas. They are willing to take chances and are prepared to discard ideas.

Significance: Children critically consider the relationship between movement composition and expression and are beginning to appreciate aesthetic qualities. They are aware of economy and clarity in movement.

Social: Movement tasks make more demands on individual and group composition. Children work unsupervised, they begin to solve their own problems and know when they need help.

9 to 10 Years

Approach: As for 9 years. Children begin to predict and plan their own work.

Body management: Children can perform movement sequences with skill.

Making dance: Children develop the notion of volume, they can manipulate spatial progression and spatial tension in shape and shaping. They develop sound and speech accompaniment for their work and can bring together an understanding of ideas from different subject media. They can use phrasing and begin to grasp the shaping of the whole dance piece.

Significance: There is an appreciation of the relationship between the parts of a movement composition and the contribution of those parts to the whole. Children can consider artistic and aesthetic qualities.

Social: The development of duo and trio work, and an understanding of possible relationships.

10 Years

Approach: As for 9 years.

Body management: Children seek to improve their skills, motivated by the demands of their compositions. They seek efficiency and sensitivity.

Making dance: Children attempt more complex compositional forms, they can handle variations of a theme.

Significance: Children begin to understand the differing feeling states expressed in movement, and they are able to consider and discuss feelings and ideas objectively.

Social: Children can accept different roles and responsibilities.

10 to 11 Years

Approach: As for 9 years.

Body management: Children practise and achieve fluency in a variety of actions and movement qualities. They can achieve good control, extension and fluent floor work. There is evidence of strong flexible movement in the body centre. Movements are completed right to the finger-tips. Action is matched with expression and commitment.

Making dance: Children create simple and complex sequences, they can recognize the essential content and recall some complex sequences with accuracy.

Significance: Children recognize the relationship between shape, dynamics, and action. They are begining to handle the interpretation of material beyond the concrete.

Social: Children work with others in both passive and active roles. They can support others whose abilities and understanding might be very different from their own.

11 Years Onward

Approach: Children can handle and combine variable actions and qualities. They can extend their reasoning and interpretation beyond the concrete. They are begining to recognize essential material and can abstract and develop ideas through dance.

Body management and making dance: Children attend to the improvement of less achieved skills. They recognize and perform variations in dynamic and spatial form and bodily manage the differences in quality. They perform small group and partner compositions and can recognize the relationship between qualities and expression in movement and in other art forms and in their environment.

Significance: The children can consider the significance of movement patterns and relate these patterns to expression and form. Children develop an awareness of form in the environment, and can begin to discuss this awareness in spoken language.

Social: Children are willing to work with others, they recognize and accept variations in ability and point of view.

Planning the Lesson

Be realistic and honest, recognize what is possible and available. It might help to begin with the answers to questions such as the following:

What can the children do?
    Not a lot, they have done little or no dance and they use the space like an adventure playground.
    Begin with simple introductory activities that are fun and safe. Either start with energetic activity with tasks that limit the space or duration, or start with no action such as drawing a still person, photographing movement, qualities of stillness.

I am not sure about teaching dance at all.
    What are you sure about? Start with that. Think about your relationship with the children or a lesson that has really caught their imagination. Build on what is already there. Magic? Wave a wand and change the space into a railway station, a spell factory, or a car breaker's dump. A visit from a policeman and his guard dog? Train the class with signals and keep a record of obedience. Adventure? Try making secret journeys or an accurate description of another's action.

Figure 7   Qualities of stillness. Begin with drawing a still person.

Where do I get ideas? I am not very imaginative.

The children are. Try brainstorming on your own or with the children. Set a simple movement task and use the children's invention. List some dance actions and add changes of moods, situations, levels, speed, place, rhythm, change of size, front, shape, number of participants. Look at art books, at exhibitions, at photographs of landscape, at sculpture and dance performance. In everyday activities watch out for likely movement ideas. Take a few risks, play movement 'consequences'.

Does dance have to be group work? The children are not good at working together.

What an opportunity! Help them by 'playing' games. Set simple tasks that require cooperation or leadership ... how many can sit on a mat without any body contact, individually occupy using one chair between three, draw a plan with one pencil between six, instruct a blindfolded partner to travel across the space with absolute safety, move in unsion without speaking, use weight support exercises

How can I get boys and girls to work together?

Is it necessary?

Thinking Through the Plan

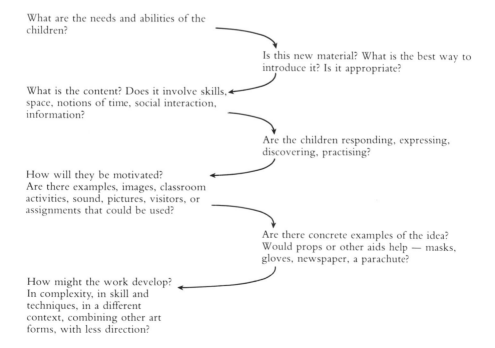

What are the needs and abilities of the children?

Is this new material? What is the best way to introduce it? Is it appropriate?

What is the content? Does it involve skills, space, notions of time, social interaction, information?

Are the children responding, expressing, discovering, practising?

How will they be motivated? Are there examples, images, classroom activities, sound, pictures, visitors, or assignments that could be used?

Are there concrete examples of the idea? Would props or other aids help — masks, gloves, newspaper, a parachute?

How might the work develop? In complexity, in skill and techniques, in a different context, combining other art forms, with less direction?

Mary Lowden

Coming Up With Ideas

If ideas do not come easily, start with anything, however ridiculous. Being irrational might excite the imagination and lead to something very workable. The following began with the idea of action and reaction:

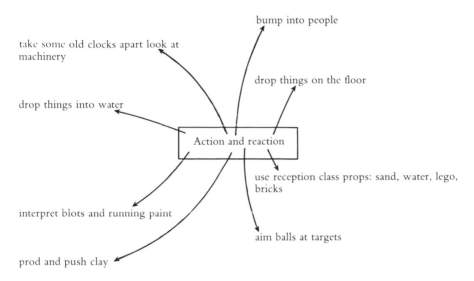

Use real examples and refer to real images to help the children find the feel and quality of movement, but clearly differentiate between the two. Imagining a leaf blown in the wind is not about being a wind-blown leaf. Watching the way smoke floats up from a candle is not about being smoke, but about capturing qualities of movement that can be seen in the smoke, and is about capturing those qualities to dance smoke or dance an expression of something that has an affinity with smoke-like movements.

image	dance action
watch crumpled plastic unfolding	uncurling with different speeds
move as if a puppet pulled by body part strings	body part leading
watching and moving with bubbles	exploring weightlessness
lifting and carrying objects	work actions
joining and separating blu-tack	meeting and parting
touching and looking at thorns and prickles	sharp pointed movement and pointed shapes

Lesson Notes

Jotted notes are often more helpful than carefully prepared plans. Be prepared with introductory activities to establish an appropriate atmosphere, outline the purpose and likely content, consider and prepare relevant props and stimulus. Plan any necessary warm-up activities so that they contribute to the lesson content by providing contrast or usable material. Stick-on memo notes can be used to draw attention to follow up ideas for the next lesson.

A general list of activities is often more appropriate for a nursery age group so that the children freely explore a range of movement ideas which can be repeated or developed as the children become familiar with the activities. Repeat the same ideas in a number of lessons, so that the children become familiar with the movements and come to 'own' them.

Examples:

activity	comment
change levels	did up/down fast. Next—add slow movement
big, small, thin, wide	repeat this sequence with rhythm
	– – –_____
jump, run, crawl	use same music, add voice?
follow me ideas	do more, perhaps change leader

Sharing and Performance

Performance is made by what happens in the space between the dancer and the spectator. The communication is a two-way dialogue and depends on a level of active giving of the self from both sides of the space. It is active sharing.

In school dance the most active sharing is likely to happen in a class lesson when the sharing is part of the learning process. The public expression of something that was private and personally experienced is nurtured and developed through activities that develop the ability to both read and see dance.

With this in mind, consider the kind of sharing that happens, say, at Christmas. At the most limited level of sharing parents come to admire their children and apart from parental pride, the criteria for spectating are often those of stage and screen cut down to size. Children should share their work with parents, but with the appropriate conditions for doing so. Either the audience is informed and knows how to look at performance in an educational context, or the performance must take on the criteria of the theatre and be as polished and professional as possible. This polishing is very time-consuming and the educational value is questionable. Witness the hours, indeed sometimes weeks of rehearsals which are more about training than learning, and in schools where timetables are normally too crowded to include the performance arts at all!

This is not to say that school dance should not be polished for performance, but the polishing must be an integral part of the doing process, and the children must be ready to acquire the skills and the understanding necessary to accept the responsibility for bringing their own work to a performance level. Indeed the art process is not complete without the editing and refinement needed for presentation. The management of body movement does not truly become dance until it has reached such a stage.

The Development of Sharing and Performance

Working in twos is a begining. The children discuss their ideas, they can appraise, coach and join movement ideas. When a child shares her movement motif with another, she has to be very clear and precise and able to verbally explain the movements as well as show them. Learning another's sequence is very different from performing one's own: one is the result of bodily sensing ideas from within, the other is sensing by watching and analyzing, the beginning of the spectator/performer dialogue.

Sharing in a group brings together individual ideas and skills and extends the variety of movement, the children begin to select and modify, to create and to consider form. Sharing also encourages the children to project their ideas and constructively appraise their work.

Sharing with another class:
This is probably the first time the children become performers. The working space becomes a stage and the performance is separated from the spectators and from the process of making. Sharing with a class that is familiar with the ideas encourages active appreciation.

Sharing with the school:
The occasion is often morning assembly. The performance must be valid both as part of the assembly and as dance.

Sharing dance with an external audience:
Are the spectators familiar with school dance in the curriculum, or do they come to see dance as they know it? Is this an opportunity to inform the audience through discussion and even workshop participation? Sit the audience within the performance space so that it becomes a teaching space rather than a theatre space.

Sharing dance using stage space:
The stage changes the performance from education to theatre which necessitates attention to skills, projection, and accuracy. Ancillary skills should be considered including programme, costume, lighting, front of house management, and sound. Theatre is magic, it is an illusion distanced from reality, theatre is another school!

Sharing in other art forms:
It is worth observing that in the sharing of school work such as visual art, the

product can be viewed in the absence of the artist. The teacher can select, mount, and display works distanced from the activity that created them. Beware that pictures, and poetry, can be presented in such a way that they serve a purpose unrelated to original intentions.

It is vital that children are given the opportunity to consider the sharing of their work and are involved in decisions about sharing as part of the arts experience. Sharing is about learning how to appreciate, how to communicate, and how to make something that is shareable.

Sharing Culture — Multicultural Education and Dance

Although a concern for multicultural influence and experience is of vital importance in education, I include only a limited reference here because it requires considerably more research and understanding than is within the scope of this book. As I see it, there are two main considerations.

The first is the culture that a child brings to the classroom. We must teach by bringing together the subject material and what the children have to offer, and be sensitive and informed about both. If the children's experience and outlook differs from our own, we must learn from the children and plan activities that allow children to contribute in their own way. This is about encouraging and showing respect for a child's response and interpretation whatever his ability, experience, and background.

The second consideration is the dance content itself, and is about understanding the place of dance within a particular culture. The arts are not independent of the way of life of a society, and movement may have far more spiritual or artistic significance in another culture than it does in our own. We understand falsely if we select bits of ritual gesture, bits of legends and bits of music without understanding what they mean within the total social and cultural structure. Understanding another culture means being immersed in it through the ceremonies, customs, legends, and so on. When these are used as 'topic' material they are by definition as patronizing and disrespectful in their superficiality. Rather than create a dance about the Christian Nativity or about Divali, create a dance about new beginnings and so encourage the children to contribute what is significant to them.

Either plan activities that are sufficiently open to encourage and value individual interpretation, or invite visitors who bring with them an expertise and belief that is valued. Being able to share, whatever the cultural background, is more important than sharing a culture.

Assessment

As teachers we are continually engaged in assessment of different kinds: appraisal, appreciation, evaluation, judgment, interpretation, analysis and marking. Assessment of skill and composition is likely to be part of the appraisal of a dance performance and include an analysis of form and interpretation of content and meaning. The evaluation of the way a child is engaged within the process of art-making should include the recognition of individual qualities — that these are nurtured and diverted as well as quantified. The assessment of skills, techniques and stored information is a fairly straightforward matter, but knowing in the arts includes feelings and attitudes. Dance forms feeling, it is created with imagination, performed with conviction, and felt experiences are shared. Assessment must therefore include the appraisal of this 'feelingness'. This is by no means easy either in the arts or in any other subject in which the affective domain is taken into account.

Subjective feeling and sensing is private and inaccessible. We can only know what those feelings are when they are evident in the outward behaviour and in the results of making and doing, as products and within products. The appreciation of a product includes liking or not liking, a 'gut' feeling that is not easy to express objectively and in words. It is however fundamentally necessary if those personal qualities and abilities that are valued in the arts are to be promoted and developed.

Although the arts are about experiences and feelings, that a person has feelings, whatever they are, does not mean that he has artistic ability. What is assessed is the appropriateness of feeling as it is seen to be expressed in the artistic form, and the skills and techniques on which that expression depends.

Assessment of an art work in the theatre or art gallery is concerned with the work itself, as when we assess the performed dance or displayed art work in school, but there is a difference. Artistic ability and aesthetic response is evident in the process as well as the product and the teacher evaluates the way a child has gone through the process, including the behaviour and attitude and experience in and beyond the art activity; the teacher evaluates the child's ability to respond, to talk, listen, notice, concentrate, be curious, to take risks, to share, to imitate, and so on. In using all this evidence the teacher must distinguish between ability and effort, between achievement and progress, and remember that in the work of very young children the sequence of image-making is often of far more significance than the final stage, and observation of the child working is frequently the *only* way to assess individual qualities and abilities.

The Assessment of a Dance Performance and of Work in Progress

A dance is not only created in the performance space but it is also created in what Peter Hall calls 'The Empty Space'. The dance is a product of what lies in front of the spectator as well as what lies behind in terms of the spectator's own experience and attention. This two-way communication creates the total dance image. The assessor is also spectating, and combines two functions each making different demands on the way the dance is attended to.

In each dance work we are confronted by the problem of form. It is this that communicates meaning and makes the artist's intentions available. Dance form is created by the way the dancer's body communicates and structures the space/time of the dance 'canvas'.

The shape and duration of a movement sets up patterns that are seen and are imagined beyond what actually exists. A gesture can create an invisible line through tension and projection, a rhythmic sequence can be suggested by but a fragment of repeated movement. When we talk about the evident formal qualities of time and space we must include those that are illusions, and appraise the 'seeming to be' qualities within the context of the whole dance.

Looking for Evidence

Assessing the forming of space
This includes shape and shaping, place and placing, mass, tension, and progression.

Low ability: The dancer is timid, movements are close to the body, the dancer avoids or lacks control in the open general space, lines and spatial structures are unclear and incomplete, design is simple and repeated without development.

High ability: Lines are clear and complete, movement relates to the unoccupied as well as to occupied space, there is an awareness of what is happening to the space, the dancer combines single and three-dimensional planes, there is concern for the visual effect of the design within the context and within the total space.

Assessing the forming of time
This includes duration, sequence, speed, rhythm and phrase.

Low ability: The beginning and end are indistinct from everyday time, duration is often too long, continuity lacks development and phrases are unclear, rhythms are inaccurate and limited, sequences show little coherence or understanding of meaning.

Assessing performance and communication
This includes space/time, force, projection, the flow of energy, the management of body energy, attention to ancillary skills such as lighting, music, props, and costume.

Low ability: The work is self-conscious, flat and uneventful; energy is lacking and uncontrolled, there is no authority or control of events, there is little to communicate, and limited understanding of what the dance is about; work is careless and indulgent.

High ability: Personal vitality commands attention and sustains interest; movements are clear and confident, reflective and immediate. The work comes across with conviction and understanding; sequences are rehearsed and polished; there is attention to the relevance and quality of ancillary elements.

Composition
This includes the structure of the dance, the relationship between the meaning and the form, clarity and appropriateness of style and interpretation, investigation and understanding of content, control, exploration and development of ideas.

Low ability: A sequence of unrelated activities; superficial and trivial content; movements have little affinity with the design or content; ideas are undeveloped and unexplored. The dancer is unaware of what is being stated; clichéd and borrowed material is reproduced with little comprehension of what is being said.

High ability: Coherent and well structured; worthwhile content that is explored with invention and enquiry. Provocative and interesting. Life is understood differently because of the dance, the dance has added something worthwhile to the experience of dancer and spectator. There is empathy and concern for what the dance is about.

Body management
Skills and techniques; strength and flexibility; fitness; alignment; vocabulary; fluency; accuracy in observation and performance; memory.

Low ability: Expression and the flow of movement is interrupted by weak management and control. The spectator is aware of the techniques; gestures are incomplete and sequences are unrelated. Concentration is not sustained and a limited vocabulary is used whatever the content, the dancer being unable to adapt, acquire or manipulate skills.

High ability: The dancer controls body weight, and is accurate and fluent in the performance of complex sequences. Phrasing is accurate and sensitive and the dancer has a wide vocabulary that can be manipulated. Footwork is precise and alignment accurate, elevation and off/on balance appear effortless. Ability is unobtrusive.

The process
Observation of the artistic process will provide evidence of other abilities and personal qualities that make up the profile of each child. Thoughtfulness, generosity, confidence and sensitivity are not known to others or assessable as private qualities, what is known about a child's thoughtfulness is known because it is evident in what is produced or done. This means that the teacher,

Figure 8   Performance ability. Individual vitality that commands attention, movements are clear and confident.

in assessing the teaching, must ask 'what am I observing?' rather than 'what am I teaching?' or, 'what are the children actually doing?', 'what does this mean in terms of what they know or can do?', 'how can another activity or a suggestion from me build on this knowing'.

In a class of children there will be a wide range of abilities and this requires that teachers not only look for abilities that are within the objectives but attend to those that are unexpected or beyond their own experience.

The list is unlimited. Consider some of the following and try to analyze the criteria for recognizing and assessing them within the different activities in and out the dance lesson. Consider also tasks and activities that promote and develop these qualities. Few learn by having information passed on from directed activities!

Thinking

The child comes up with ideas, can follow an idea through and find the appropriate movement, can recognize ideas as they emerge through movement and take note of body sensing in developing form with understanding. The child can 'see' the next sequence in relation to the whole idea and search for the right movement, rejecting and changing 'wrong' ones and incorporating existing movements with new plans.

Social skills

The child is able to listen and respond to the ideas of others, can interrelate with tolerance, sensitivity or leadership, values other ideas and experiences, will take up and support another's idea, is aware of personal contribution within the group dynamics, and can work alone and knows when to.

Communication

The child can talk and listen, explain ideas and feelings, discuss, question, consider, compare, analyze, support, represent and communicate and manipulate in written and dance form, using visual images, symbols, and design.

Awareness and attention

The child notices with interest and feeling, observes and investigates, values experiences, seeks out information and skills, sustains interest even through chore stages, is appropriately involved and works with conviction. The child can complete and refine work, critically appraise her own work and that of others, and is aware of standards and values.

Self-image

The child is aware and understands experiences, values self as a contributing factor, is adventurous and accepts failure as part of the process, knows her limitations, and contributes when there is something to contribute.

The ability to see what is evident in each child's work and behaviour is developed through experienced looking, by sharing observations and through investigative reading. As the dance activity is happening try to watch just what the children are doing and listen to their comments. Is there evidence here of enquiry, imagination, and understanding? Make time to participate as an observer. If you have a student taking the class use this opportunity to 'read' the children, to watch HOW they work. Is talk involved, and if so, with whom, and what kind of talk? In written work, instead of marking completed work, look at the way a child approaches writing, at where he looks for ideas and how he puts the words together. How does the child edit? With a rubber? By crossing out? By keeping and comparing different attempts? In the dance lesson, how does he find movements? By watching others? By waiting for direction? By being completely immersed in the bodily experience? Through spontaneous response? On what bases are ideas selected?

Objective evaluation is an essential part of the children's dance experience. In the following example of students' work, the opportunity to evaluate was part of the process of making dance, and included evaluation of the content and ways of working.

As a starting point, the students reviewed work already done in order to consider possible development. They listed available resources that would focus attention on a relevant and worthwhile idea. A chance visit to a nearby car dump and the experience of seeing a car squashed into a rectangle of metal had stimulated ideas about making and destroying things. Research included talking to the workmen at the dump, taking photographs and collecting information about the process of resalvaging metal and about making cars.

The students considered various ways of sharing the information and what they felt about the dump. The shape of the crumpled metal and the sound of the crusher stimulated movement ideas that captured the power of a motor car which was crushed so easily. As the work developed the destruction idea became tedious and students found that by reversing some of the movement motifs they could reverse the process and add the notion of construction to destruction.

The project included constant evaluation of purpose, content, and dance-making. Students reviewed their body skills and sought advice and practise, they used spectators and video film to compare the feel of the movement with how it looked, and to consider transitions and sequence. It was also important for them that the content was understood by others as they came to feel quite strongly about caring for things and caring for the environment. They had to tease out what was essential and find a way of expressing this in movement with clarity and intensity. This meant a continuous questioning of their understanding and feelings as well as a rejection of any movements that did not seem to fit.

This project also led to an evaluation of the learning situation which included the following considerations: What sustained the interest in the project? What was the level and content of individual participation, and could this be improved? What was learnt about dance and what was learnt about making cars and recycling physical resources? In the light of what was successful or unsuccessful, what should follow? What needs, interests and abilities became apparent? What was the teacher's role? What was the level of enquiry and understanding?

Evaluating Dance Performance

The ability to see what is evident in a dance performance is developed through experience and study. This seeing needs thoughtful preparation especially if there is only one performance. Before assessing a dance, list the qualities you expect or hope to find. Try to see the dance thoroughly, allow a few minutes before the dance to prepare yourself, focus in on the situation, empty the mind of any distractions, get into a receptive frame of mind, be open and ready to concentrate on whatever is to come. Have a notepad to jot down any words or marks that will assist the recall, but do this without taking your eyes off the dance.

As soon as the dance is finished, write down key words and clarify any points with the dancers. Allow that you might have misread or overlooked something. If possible freely discuss your initial response with other assessors. As soon as possible concentrate on a recall of the dance as remembered, and think. It is surprising how much can be recalled of the dance performance and of your initial response. 'Read' through the whole experience in the imagination; be honest and pay attention to what you saw, not what you thought you saw. Above all, concentrate, try to unravel the structure, review the skills, note moments of interest and excitement.

Write a critique and compare it with that of others. Discuss different and similar findings, exchange reasons and interpretations; there will be differences in the appeal of the dance, but informed and considered assessments generally agree.

As teachers we also have to recognise the possible long-term effect of the work we plan and implement, the awakening of interests and establishing of principles that may only become apparent long after the children have left school. Although we must evaluate activities according to the immediate evidence and can see what a child is achieving within the context of certain situations, we must also plan our work and develop our teaching abilities based on a faith in the children we teach and a faith in our own vision and understanding.

Perhaps more important than any assessment procedures is the awareness that there are dances that transcend all the analysis, that go beyond any need to look at skills or structures, that fulfil what they are. Enjoy them, they are dance, and nothing more needs to be said!

4
Ideas for Lessons

Introduction

The dance lesson, like any other teaching, must have a sense of purpose, but only the teacher can really identify the point of the lesson. For this reason I have omitted any reference to objectives. The lessons are intended as prompts for ideas and ways of working rather than recipes for achievement. I have used these ideas with children of different ages and with adults, and although I have indicated an age range the content can be modified according to ability and context. Generally speaking, the lessons for the 5+ child or lessons that are introductory provide foundation material for any age.

The lessons are grouped to facilitate reference but the material should not be bounded by the lesson or timetable. In order to give a range of movement vocabulary and subject matter I have tried to avoid duplicating material, but there must inevitably be some overlap, and when using these lessons it should be remembered that, in learning and teaching, ideas are continually reinforced or reinterpreted so that understanding is an accumulation of knowledge and experience.

Much of the movement content includes reference to other subject matter so that the dance lesson becomes an effective and integral part of the school day and the whole curriculum rather than a preparation for a dance vocation. The final lesson about migration is an example of a structure that could be used for any historical or documentary material including local history or current events. Likewise, the water lesson shows the contribution of movement study in science or environmental studies. This brings me to two important points. The first is that the subject matter must become more available BECAUSE it is learnt through movement, movement must be an appropriate way in, thus the lesson about food deals with the form and structure of food and not with the economics of its production or with nutrition. The second point is that dance is NOT about children being machines or plants or animals, it is about observing and becoming aware of structure and movement in the environment, and exploring those qualities as part of the human movement of dance language.

Although they are labelled as lessons, the ideas do not fit into a twenty-minute slot but vary from short exercises to what might be half a term's work. For simplicity I have addressed the lessons to both 'you' the teacher and 'you' the children, but the difference should be clear. No difference is intended between him and her, so whichever I have used, read either.

Body Awareness

Lesson 1: Body Sensing; Management of the Body; Body Weight (5+)

A quiet undisturbed environment is necessary, which might be easier to find in the classroom. If space is limited children can rest on chairs or tables or on any available floor space.

Lying still, listen to sounds. For children who find stillness and quiet a new experience this will need practice. Concentrate on the sounds, imagine what is happening, in your mind try to imagine what you hear. Quietly describe the sounds and the images to a partner. The teacher may add sounds by tapping, humming, walking, handling paper. Recorded sounds are best avoided as they sound electronic and are often distorted and require recognition rather than interpretation.

Use the same kind of concentration to become aware of the body; of the contact with the floor; note parts of the body that press on the floor; parts that hurt; parts not touching; parts in contact with other parts of the body. How do you know this? How does skin on skin feel? Clothing on skin? Air on skin?

Imagine the shape of the body; change the shape and imagine how it looks. Consider the distance between the hands and the feet.

Become aware of breathing: feel as if the out breath flows out through the toes, the fingers, the top of the head. Accompany the rise and fall with a movement of the hands; of the head; of the torso. Use the movement to sit and gradually to stand.

Lying on the floor, stand, removing one part of the body at a time — no part may touch the floor once removed. Reverse the process to lie down.

Support the weight on knees/feet/hands/bottom/one foot/shoulder/fingers and toes/one elbow and one knee.

This play with weight support encourages the children to think of dance as any bodily movement without the limitation of being on the feet as in folk and social dance.

Change weight support suddenly and gradually.
Explore large and small shapes using different weight support.

Select three such positions, create a sequence and repeat it exactly. Observe and copy a partner's sequence. Add the two together. Try to perform the sequence in reverse order. Use the sequence to travel, modifying as necessary.

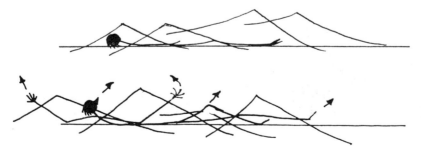

Lesson 2: Moving Body Parts; Using Newspaper (5+)

This lesson needs sufficient paper for each child to have four large sheets, but take care because the print can show on immaculate white T-shirts!

The use of newspaper is fun and encourages an awareness of self without self-consciousness.

Lying on the floor, each child covers himself completely in sheets of newspaper. Feeling invisible contributes to the focus on self. The teacher uses a tambour to suggest secretive movement. Gradually move isolated parts of the body to emerge without controlling the paper ... as it falls, the paper makes an interesting sound. Allow fingers/a hand/knee/nose/toe/shoulder/bottom to emerge into the outside space.

Figure 9   Body awareness. Isolated parts of the body emerging from under a covering of newspaper.

Figure 10

Lie on the fallen newspaper as if it were a raft using less and less of the surface of the paper. Let separate body parts creep off the 'raft' onto the floor.

Shape the paper and lie on it so that the body is shaped by the paper; shape the paper for a partner; share one shape of paper.

Watch as the teacher slowly tears down one sheet, listen to the tearing sound (this could be amplified with a microphone). Observe the separation. Make a whole body shape, use the sound of tearing paper to 'tear' one body part away. Join with a partner and repeat, make each tear last as long as possible and develop the resulting shapes.

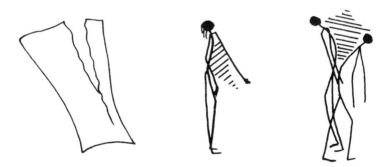

Crumple a sheet of paper; copy the action and the shape with the body ... slowly unfold to become flat. Repeat, change speed and change the parts of the body that move first and last.

Join with a partner to become crumpled and unfolded.

Voice work: Children read any extract in the paper ... silently, loudly, decreasing and increasing volume, as if important; angry; bored; excited; use readings to accompany movement.

In twos, use newspaper to construct an image: sunbathing; a picnic; a machine; shipwreck; a king. Give a time limit and only suggest titles if necessary, let the paper itself suggest ideas.

85

Lesson 3: Body Parts Leading; Being a Puppet (5+)

Introductory activity: puppets

Lying flat on the floor, imagine strings attached from each body part to the ceiling which pull the parts up. The teacher directs with sound and/or voice to sustain the movement: 'knee being pulled up ... up ... up ... and hold ... relax.' Allow the rest of the body to cooperate whilst retaining the relationship with the floor as if in opposition. Try nose; toe; elbow; bottom; tummy; ear; heel; rib cage.

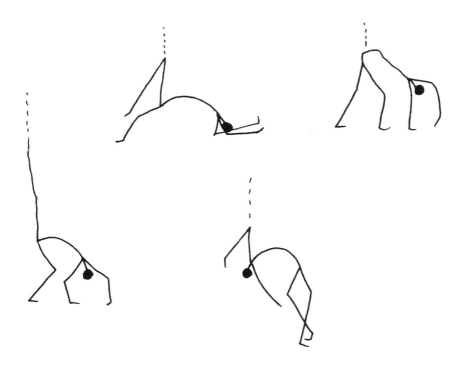

Introductory activity: puppets

Development

Add an accent at beginning of each movement using even phrasing:

$$|1 \quad 2 \quad 3 \quad 4|2 \quad 2 \quad 3 \quad 4|3 \quad 2 \quad 3 \quad 4|4 \quad 2 \quad 3 \quad 4|$$
$$\text{high} \qquad \text{deep} \qquad \text{side} \qquad \text{forward}$$

or uneven phrasing:

$$|1|2 \quad 2 \quad 3 \quad 4 \quad 5 \quad 6|3 \quad 2|4 \quad 2 \quad 3 \quad 4|$$
$$\text{high} \qquad \text{deep} \qquad \text{side} \quad \text{forward}.$$

Work with a partner as if the two bodies were one. Use one body part to lead a shared action.

Figure 11   Imagining head and hands being pulled up and up by a puppet master.

Alternatively select two body parts that lead in opposite directions, move as far as possible without losing contact or near contact.

Use the same bodily sensation, but imagine parts are pulled in other directions: downward, sideways. Reach as far as possible but retain the opposition.

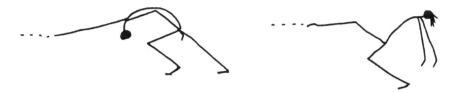

Use the top of the head to lift the body; the bottom to move downwards; elbow/ear/rib cage to move to the side; chest to move forwards; middle of the back to move backwards.

Change the direction of movement, explore the effect of using different parts to move: deep; high right; high left; deep forward; high back; deep right forward.

Repeat some of the movements as large as possible with maximum extension, travelling if necessary.

Repeat as small as possible feeling the slight movement in the body centre rather than in the extremities.

Group work

Make a contracted group shape, use *one* body part to lead the group into an extended shape ... as if unwinding a reel of cotton.

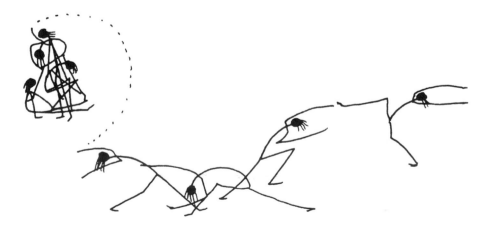

Create a sequence in which the group unwinds and rewinds. Vary the lead using end and middle parts.

Refer to folk dances that use winding and unwinding formations. Observe natural winding structures: young ferns, shells, caterpillars.

Development. See Focus Lessons 34, 35, 36.

Pathways and Shape

Introduction

Shape in the real world suggests the fixed shape of objects. Shape in dance happens through movement: shapes progress in time so that shapes have pathways.

Pathways in dance include: the floor pattern of travel; the pathway of bodily gesture; the pathway of focus; the pathway of the transitional movements that are made between one shape and another.

Lesson 4: The Pathway of Gesture; Giving and Taking; Ritual and Ceremony (6+)

The shaping of such a movement in dance contributes to the form and the meaning so that pathways need to be clearly defined. Gestures in dance are not confined to the hands and head and are performed by any body part including the feet, legs, and torso. The following ideas can be adapted to use other body parts.

Introduction: gesture

Use everyday gestures to discover the shape of giving, taking, giving directions, rejecting, protecting, and sharing.

Concentrate on giving or offering, and perform the action with different expression:

'Have this, I don't want it.'
'I would like to give you this.'
'Is this any use to you?'
'Take this away from me.'
'Look after this for me.'

Observe and note the differences.

Explore the effect of change in level, direction, focus, speed, relationship to the body, amount of body used, the flow of the movement, duration, and stillness.

Use one idea, enlarge and refine the movement, add before and after gestures which may require stepping or change of weight support.

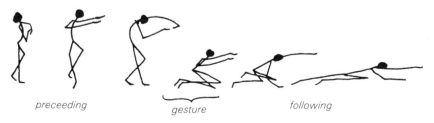

preceeding   *gesture*   *following*

Repeat this process using a 'taking' action. Explore the difference between: grabbing as if a number of £5 notes had dropped from the sky; grabbing before others have a chance; selecting with curiosity and wonder; receiving something desperately needed; accepting an unwanted gift.

Select and refine a 'taking' gesture, and add the movement to the gesture of offering to create a sequence: ABA. With a partner, work together to reciprocate these two gestures. Pay particular attention to the transitional pathway between gestures, and note how the transition colours the statement.

Ritual gestures

Observe and study ritual gestures using film and photographs as well as everyday observation. Examples are: a hand in marriage; a coronation; flowers at a funeral; sporting and academic awards; handshakes and embraces; official welcome and opening ceremonies.

Using a small object such as a pebble, create a group ceremonial sequence that gives the pebble much significance. Consider: dignity and importance; repetition; group formation and unity. Choreograph the study to music—slow movements from Handel or Vivaldi are possible accompaniments.

Lesson 5: The Shape of Travel; a Shape Score (5+)

Follow a score by reading the structure of the hall or classroom wall. Follow the shape of the windows, roof supports, furniture, drapery, or the shapes in a picture.

Other score ideas

The figure 1 suggests straight lines and angles,
       2 suggests twists and spirals,
       3 suggests curves and circles.

Listen to the melody line in a piece of familiar music, for example, Brahms' Lullaby. Draw the melody and use it as a dance score, add dance to melody exactly matching or developing the shape.

Extract a section of a drawing or painting, either a reproduction or children's work.

Example: Following a dance lesson, children paint the floor patterns they remember. A section of this painting becomes a score:

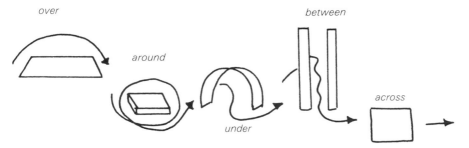

The score is used for dance and for music-making to accompany the dance.

Similar starting points can derive from rubbings, leaf patterns, knots and stitching, wood grain, or string printing.

The shape of travel and the shape of floor patters

Develop an awareness of pattern by imagining the feet leaving a trail, or better still make paint footprints along sheets of lining paper, or follow gym floor markings or pavement squares.

Trail patterns are often determined by obstacles as when a footpath goes around a fallen tree. Use the gym apparatus as obstacles, discover the floor patterns that follow including change of level or action.

Record some of these patterns and use them for making dance without the obstacles.

Draw the journey to school noting hazards and obstacles on particular routes: Create routes around the classroom furniture and make up rules of travel. This might well extend into a maths project investigating purpose and efficiency.

Observe and record the pathways of snails, minibeasts, a cat, the postman, and people shopping.

Investigate ritual pathways such as processional routes, find out why there are such routes and investigate labyrinth. See Lesson 45. Observe habitual routes in school such as entering the playground or the classroom. Observe and analyze pathways in organized games and in the playground. Learn some of the pathway patterns in country dance and find out their origins. Discover the resultant pathway of performing a movement sequence such as hop-run-turn-balance-fall.

Follow a leader, explore interweaving and merging pathways. Join different pathways to make a dance study, and consider continuity; interrupted flow; phrasing; start and finish.

Structure a pathway pattern to follow a piece of music, emphasize the phrasing with changes of direction or pattern. The following example uses Bach's Brandenburg Concerto No. 3:

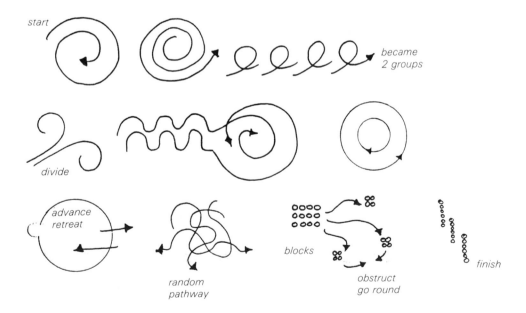

Pathway variations: Divide, join, reverse, inverse, contain, surround, fill, meander, advance, retreat, surprise, repeat, become more, become less, accuracy, random, opposition, unity.

Mary Lowden

Lesson 6: Thinness and Flatness (5–6)

Using a sheet of paper, each child explores its thinness and flatness. This includes seeing, touching and describing. Examine the paper as it lies flat, leans or stands. Tissue paper and card will show the effect of different paper strengths.

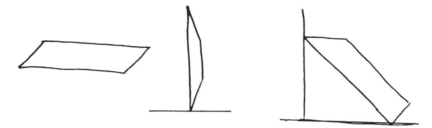

Using the paper as reference, explore the body as a thin, flat thing.

Paper thinness can be folded so that it rests or hangs. Thinness becomes three-dimensional

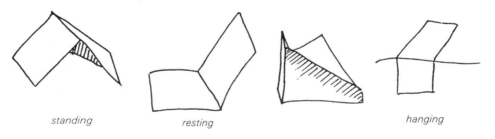

standing   resting   hanging

as does the body

or groups of flat bodies

Tear the paper into strips: the thin paper divides into thin, narrow pieces.

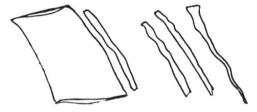

Similarly the body can divide into two.

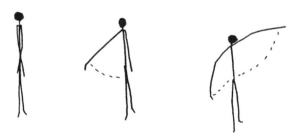

Groups of 'thin' bodies can separate into thin bits and rejoin. Use the sound of tearing paper as accompaniment. Discuss the feel and look of the separation ... is it easy, willing, tough, uncomfortable? How do these feelings affect the movement? Is the tearing gradual or sudden, jerky or smooth?

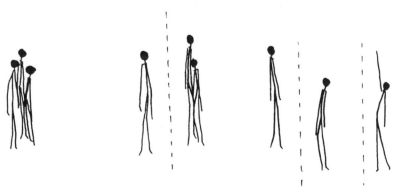

Figure 12   Tearing paper into strips to explore thinness.

Thin strips of paper can take on different shapes, for example when wound around a pencil. Introduce words like cylinder; roll; curl; coil; enlace.

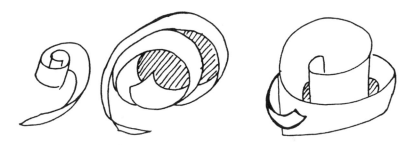

Explore individual and group movement in and out of the curl, to twist, turn, spiral, and unwind.

Return to the sheet of flat paper, crumple it and notice and describe the shape ... note shadow and in front and behind shapes.

Crumple a plastic sheet, watch as it is released, note different speeds, levels, place and shape as it changes. Use this observation to create a sequence of movement.

Development: Add words to describe and accompany the sequence. Use the words to make a crumple poem. Find sounds to accompany the movement. Make a sound/dance/poem sequence.

Reverse the sequence so that the dance folds and unfolds.

Repeat but extend the size as much as possible so that parts have to separate while retaining the sense of the whole.

Look for objects that are flat but bent, curled and twisted. How much energy was required to change the flatness; and to show that energy in the movement?

Lesson 7: Geometric Shape and Transformation (7–13)

Introduction
In the past we have tended to cling to notions of stability and to understand objects and events as separate entities with fixed relationships and unchanging rules. This is a misconception of our environment and of life itself.

The following dance work introduces the notion that shapes differ and become different, and contributes to a classification of shape that includes elasticity, rigidity, and transformation. The movement enables children to feel the qualities of shape bodily, to create three-dimensional shapes, and to explore the nature of change.

Figure 13   Bodily sensing shape and changing shape.

Movement example
Children join hands in threes. Explore ways of making triangles out of three bodies. What happens if the size of the sides change or the angles are squashed?

What happens if you work with four, five or six people?

Change the triangle into a rhombus or a circle. Change the size and place of the triangle.

Fragment the triangle into pieces and rejoin them. What shape should the 'pieces of body' be if they are recognizable as bits of a triangle?

Make a triangle with the whole class. Can it be turned round, inverted, shrunk, stretched, or squashed?

In groups, play with changing shapes whilst preserving the number of bodies; the number of sides; the size.

Discover shapes that occur in the outside world. What shapes are difficult to describe, and why? What makes the shape of things change — spaghetti when cooked; plants without water; fruit going bad; china broken; shadows in the playground?

How can we record the shapes and changes of shape in a movement lesson so that they can be repeated exactly a week later? This introduces the use of symbols (see Notation in Chapter Five). Finding words and symbols contributes to the development of concepts and gives experience meaning.

Mary Lowden

Movement study: autumn — transformation of shape — leaves
Each child has an autumn leaf for observation. Draw and describe the shape exploring words: wilted, twisted curled, warped, crinkly, wrinkled, holed, sharp, brittle, jagged, rolled.

Match the shape with body shape, change the front, point of view, level, and place, but maintain the shape.

Imagine the same leaf in early summer, and find words to describe it then.

Add this imagined shape to your existing body leaf shape so that you have a past and present. Imagine the present leaf further decayed and add this shape. Refine the whole sequence making sure that all body parts are involved and that the change of shape is continuous consider duration and speed: there may be moments when the leaf suddenly curls or falls.

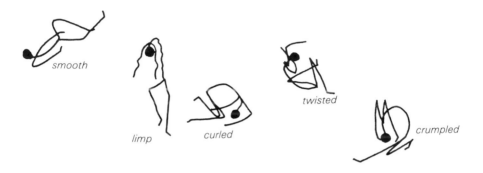

smooth

limp   curled   twisted   crumpled

In small groups, share the observation of leaf shapes and discuss the work so far. Create a group study, each contributing an individual sequence, modified if necessary. Take it in turns to watch and direct the study. Refine and perform.

Create a sound sequence to accompany the study, using words and feelings to describe the changes that occur. If necessary record the sound or create sound for another group. The word sequence might become a poem or piece of prose.

Using Space

Introduction

The large empty space in a hall or gymnasium can be overwhelming for the teacher and the children and so affect the behaviour and attitude. Space is the 'canvas' for the movement expression and projection, and its use needs practice, familiarity, encouragement, and sensitive planning. Begin with what feels safe and easy. You don't have to use the hall period if the children are not ready to use the hall space.

100

Lesson 8: Working in a Small Space (Any Age)

Start by using limited space and section off the floor space using chairs or ropes. Reduce the space still further by finding the least space possible that the class or group can occupy without touching.

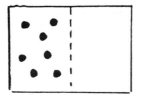 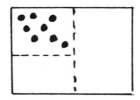 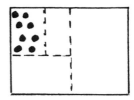

Challenge groups to share a hoop, a mat, or a sheet of newspaper. Explore movement tasks within this confined space. (Those who find this difficult can work alone or in twos.) Change places; change body weight, make contrasting or identical body shapes, include sudden or slow transitions, make group statues to interpret given or chosen subjects.

Travel within a crowded space as if others are infectious/spies/suspected enemies.

Allow time and give plenty of encouragement. Focus on the task and do not draw attention to those who find this difficult.

Use gym mats as imaginary rafts in a shark-infested sea, or as magic carpets. The mats provide a limited space to share; add imagination to spark off ideas for movement and creative writing. For example: from the mat describe the scene as if you had been shipwrecked, or flying over a city in a storm. Use the lesson and the imagined situations to learn about getting out the mats!

Figure 14   A group of children share the limited space on a sheet of newspaper.

Each child works with a chair either in the classroom or in the hall, the chair provides a home base and some kind of security. Find different ways of sitting on the chair, of standing and approaching the chair. Look at picture reproductions for ideas about context and character. What is the person feeling? Where is he? What is about to happen? Imitate the posture, imagine the position before and after, join the movements to make a phrase. Write a script to accompany the phrase.

Use three different pictures. Find appropriate transitions to move from one similar shape to another. Can your partner find your starting picture?

These movement studies can be used to support studies of people and events in drama, literature, history, art appreciation and drawing.

Examples of reproductions
Cézanne: *The card players*; *Woman with coffee pot*.
Tintoretto: *Portrait of Jacopo Sansovino*; *A Venetian senator*.
Modigliani: *Girl with brown hair*.
Leonardo da Vinci: *Mono Lisa*.
Augustus John: *Gwen John with a parasol*; *Self-portrait*.
Rembrandt: Various self-portraits.

Lesson 9: Getting Used to a Large Space (Any Age)

Find a space, mark it by noticing the floor marks; turn, lie, jump, reach, make the space your own by building a newspaper 'wall'. Find the limits of your own space 'bubble'. Does this cross or overlap any one else's 'bubble'? Can you share the space without touching others or getting in the way? Move around the hall space whilst defining your space.

Return to your starting position, leave it and return to it as if: unwilling, cautious, pulled, pushed, enticed, exploded; one body part at a time.

Travel away from this spot and visit every part of the general space. Return to your spot. Repeat the travel pathway exactly. Can you remember it?

Figure 15   Marking one's own personal space with a boundary of newspaper.

Figure 16   Leaving the newspaper space using one body part at a time.

Repeat the journey — moving very fast; with different actions; with pauses; using different levels; and repeat. Watch someone else's pattern and repeat what you saw. Was it accurate?

From a starting point, select two other locations, travel to each and return.

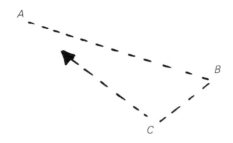

Vary the pathway, then the action and the speed.

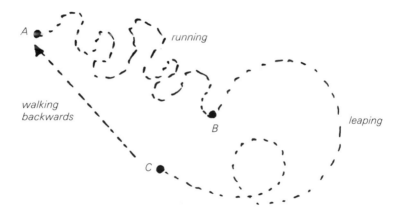

Development

Follow a partner's pathway; reverse the journey; add rhythm and phrase using music.

Crossing the space (N.B. Take into account the hazards of walls, windows, stacked chairs and general walkways.)

Clear an empty space and all stand at the edge. If necessary define the space with chalk or spotlight.

All must cross the space twice with no more or less than two moving at a time. Add different tasks:

- Cross the space as if afraid; injured; in a hurry; lost.
- Cross the space as if it is cold; hot; slippery; a lion's den.
- Cross the space using movements that are large; grotesque; angular; funny; floppy.

These tasks are for spontaneous improvisation so prepare a good list of ideas and use them according to the response. Encourage but do not insist on equal participation as some children enjoy this more than others but all learn form watching.

Development

Cross the space individually or in small groups to introduce the feel of performance and opportunity for critical observation. This is a way of working common to dance technique classes but should only be used in school when the children have sufficient ability and confidence.

A technique class use of space

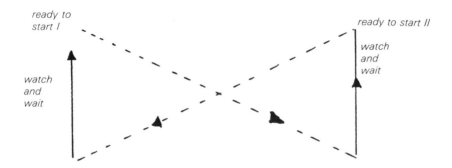

Ways of moving across this space (see also Lessons 40 and 41):

Travel: free running, running to a count, running fast. Using hands and feet, no feet, crawl, roll, hop, skip, gallop.

Change the body support, using a count of 8, and be ready to repeat the sequence on the next count.

Crossing the space
8 counts and a change of level

Stepping: long steps, high steps, tiny steps. Stepping backwards, sideways, in a pattern.

Change the level of stepping with even count:

Travel using a given sequence, for example: turn, step, lift, and roll.

Travel using a movement score, a rhythm, a music phrase.

Travel as if: hungry; ill; important; unwilling; dejected; following a map or directions.

Travel in groups that are: identical in movement; carrying a shared burden; helping each other; prisoners tied together; in a procession.

Development: a landscape study

Consider the line of the horizon in a rural landscape. Use black and white photographs and geological investigation. Use these shapes to create a travelling pathway. Cross the space in a zig-zag pattern to extend the duration of the movement. Use a photograph as a score.

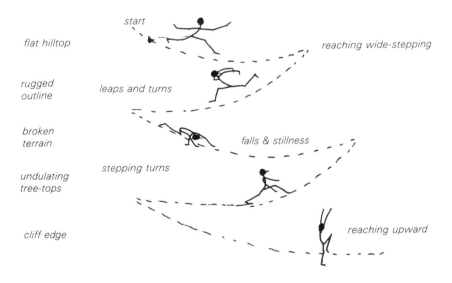

Lesson 10: The Space In Between; Making and Moving in Holes (7–13)

Space is shaped by what happens in and around it. Children need practice to see the shape between things as well as the shape of things themselves.

Start by drawing.

Pile up some chairs to make a 'still life'. Draw attention to the spaces between the legs and backs. It helps if the chairs are balanced at unusual angles.

Use large sheets of sugar paper and charcoal or crayon to draw the shapes of these spaces.

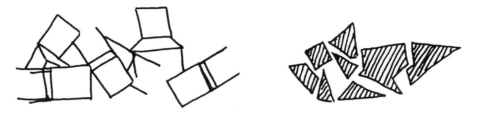

Trace the shapes so that they can be cut out in black paper and mounted on white paper. Repeat the original composition. The effect is exciting and the success reinforces awareness of the spaces.

Observe and discuss the spaces made by objects in the classroom. Note how the shape of space changes according to the viewpoint. We do not necessarily share the same view of the world!

Movement

Each child is with a chair. If possible rest the chair, carefully, on its side or back, and occupy the space within the structure.

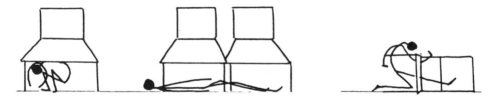

Repeat these actions without the chair. Move as if within the same confined space.

Make hole shapes with the body, holes can be completed or suggested.

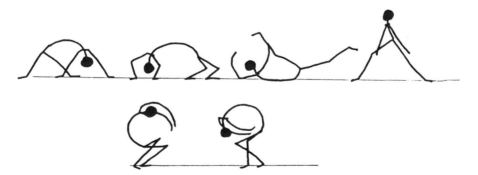

In twos, make holes and occupy the partner's body 'holes', without bodily contact.

As a group make a combination of hole shapes for another group to pass through. Be as cooperative as possible.

Two groups travel across the space, alternatively making hole shapes and passing through.

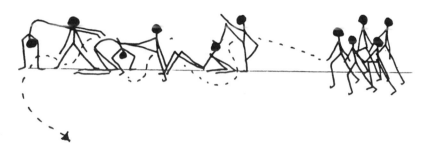

A group meet the solid block of *B* group. Holes open and close again to allow group *A* to pass through as in a liquid.

A group stands in a dispersed formation creating hole pathways. As group *B* passes through, these holes are disturbed and they fall, turn, sway, reassume position or remain changed as wind passing through grass.

Development

Filling and outlining space is very significant within the language of dance.

Imagine a large hole in the dance space, move around the edge with caution, be repelled when too near.

Become trapped in an imaginary space, try every way to escape with no success.

Move within the space 'hole' as if the boundary increases and decreases, appears and disappears.

Move within the space as if its shape continually changes by being flat, thin, long, round, low, tall.

Work with a partner as if one were within and one without; try to make contact or avoid any relationship.

Watch these movements and discuss possible meanings. What do movements say about the space or about the dancers.

Interpret a story, a situation a word or sound, using some of these movement ideas. Use lines from poetry, e.g.:

I am not yet born; O hear me (Louis Macneice)

Time held me green and dying
Though I sang in my chains like the sea (Dylan Thomas)

Social Sensitivity: Working With Others

Introduction

Social interaction is an essential element in the performing arts of drama, music and dance. Work in each provides the opportunity and the necessity to work together objectively and cooperatively. If children find working together difficult, do not complain but do something about it. Teach them with encouragement and evidence of success. Focus on the task and NOT ON THE INABILITY. Social interaction in dance means sharing the materials of dance and that does mean the space, the ideas and bodies.

Lesson 11: The Personal Space; Sharing Space (Any Age)

Begin by establishing an awareness of personal space, the kinesphere. This is the space that the body occupies; it is like a bubble around the body that can be invaded or shared by those who come close. Observe groups of people to study body posture and gestures that include or exclude others. What movements are used to establish the 'right' amount of space between the self and others and in what circumstances?

crowded 'bubbles'

separate 'bubbles'

Introductory movement

Sitting still anywhere but in a space by yourself. Stay still long enough to feel as if you possess that spot, quietly leave it and return. If this is difficult begin with a chair. Choose several 'spots' and sit in each avoiding others as much as possible. Choose when to move yourself.

Sit beside another's spot who then has to do the same, rather like a slow version of musical chairs.

Practise this in the classroom by sitting in another's place.

As you come into the hall for the lesson sit in a class or group formation that is prescribed, move to accommodate others, and try this without speaking at all.

Stillness

The sense of stillness is a dance quality requiring the confidence and concentration to occupy a space with assurance, it is to movement what silence is to sound in music and involves the ability to listen. Stillness and silence are qualities unfamiliar to many children used to the continuous background of recorded music and they need the time and opportunity to appreciate both.

For this reason the following activities should be done a little and often.

Find ways of being still and comfortable.

Sit or lie still, relaxed and calm. Concentrate on the sounds around. Listen to your breathing. Sustain stillness for a measured time using a sand timer and the calling of the register. How long is this and can it last longer?

Recall those sounds in your memory, compare them with yesterday's sounds or those your partner heard. Record them in drawing or writing.

Listen to someone walking. Can you tell if the sound is near or going away? Listen to music, a poem, a conversation, and imagine the scene or the people.

Travel and then stop still to a sound accompaniment. Can you be still immediately? Make sure you are in balance. Practice still body positions that are quick to make and hold, measure the duration. Try difficult changes of level and weight support. Direct your own move/still sequence, this means that others will move when you are still and needs the confidence to be conspicuous. Add increase and decrease in speed and change of action.

Remain still as a group while the rest of the class are very active around you. Several groups move in rotation. Very active children can have more active turns!

Alternate the hands, one moving and one still.

In twos alternate movement and stillness; repeat as groups.

Play statue games, from continuous movement freeze when directed, to be like a doormat, a post, a prickly bush, a frightened cat, a flash of lightening.

Repeat in small groups to make statues that could be: a picnic, a bus queue, a shipwreck, a bird table, putting up a tent, a wedding photograph. Immediacy and stillness are important, rather than accuracy or brilliant invention, so allow no time for discussion and alteration.

112

Using short pieces of music, move or remain still to the sound or the silence. Make statue groups for the others to move through and around.

Development
Incorporate stillness in dance studies and consider the individual contribution. Watch for stillness in dance on film. Watch the people in the background in a television or stage performance.

Lesson 12: Sharing Movement and Making Body Contact (7–13)

Society has reservations about bodily contact and even holding hands is only acceptable in particular circumstances. This is a natural shyness that should be respected. Contact in dance is part of the medium and is about the relationship between two bodies rather than two people. The introduction of such contact must be as objective as possible. (For more information, investigate Japanese martial arts, and Body Contact Improvisation.)

Sharing and trusting: movement
In twos, explore ways of taking each other's weight, move from one idea to another with control and utmost care for your partner, maintaining flow and momentum.

In groups, support, carry, and position one body; all cooperate including the 'body'.

Recall gymnastic activities such as leapfrog and balances.

Roll across a lying down group, and lie on a rolling group.

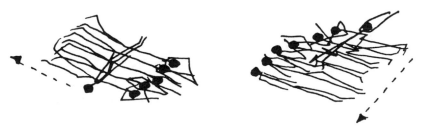

113

Move towards a focus passing whoever is in the way by crawling over or under them (see Lessons 34 and 35).

In groups, have body contact with at least one other person. How far can the group move along; up; outwards?

Construct a single sculpture with several bodies; move from one sculpture to another.

Create sculpture images by putting a partner's body in place. Discover possible titles or answer given titles. Repeat with one 'sculptor' using several bodies. Develop this by adding phrasing to counts or to music.

Lesson 13: Leading and Following (7–13)

This is an introduction to taking responsibility or for giving up one's own idea to support another's.

Follow a partner's travel actions, change leader.

Lead a partner with a gentle hand hold; partner closes eyes. Develop the pathway by changing the level and direction. Lead a seeing partner, change the leadership without speech. Repeat without actually touching.

Share body shapes and movements by matching, complementing, joining, interrelating.

Figure 17 Joining and interrelating body shapes and movements.

115

In groups make a starting group formation: a block, a line, an arrow, a circle. Explore the action and interaction between groups such as an arrow splitting a group or a circle surrounding a group. How many situations can develop without organization and discussion?

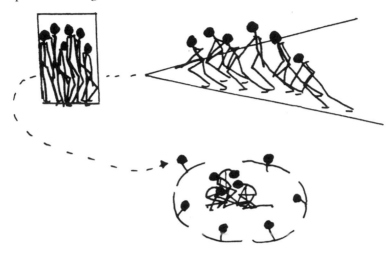

Children should use each other as critical spectators whenever they are creating movements or sequences of movement. There should be plenty of opportunity to combine selected movement ideas including editing and coaching.

Choreograph a dance for other performers. Extend the task to include musicians and a producer.

Work separately on a common idea and then combine them.

Create a group study in which each member contributes a variation. Variations can be performed together or in order. A musical accompaniment may require very accurate timing.

matching   *contrasting*   *joining*   *inter relating*

Create a sequence to combine stillness and movement. Perform with each taking the opposite role:

A	still	move	still
B	move	still	move

Repeat using different actions:

A	high	deep	high
B	deep	high	deep

A	round	angular	round
B	angular	round	angular

Weight and force

Lesson 14: Sensing weight, force in movement (6–13)

The measured weight of objects is absolute weight and although this can be used in dance, weight or force in dance is virtual weight or the relative weight sensed in the body and seen in the way the body moves. Mime creates an illusion of weight, the body looks as if it is dealing with something of a particular weight.

Although absolute weight, relative weight and mimed weight can all be used in dance, they should not be confused. Trying to push the piano and using a pushing action in dance is not the same thing, but the experience of sensing real weight can contribute to movements that have a weight quality. To be aware of how much body weight we carry, children can weigh each other and support each other.

Sensing weight: experiencing forcefulness with a partner.

pushing

and pulling

Figure 18   Supporting each other's weight.

Pushing against the floor/wall/heavy object, note the shape and the posture of the body by watching and repeating the position.

Push against an imaginary wall.

Pull on an imaginary rope.

Imagine you are shut in an iron box, push up and out to escape with different body parts, maintain the pressure as you increase the size of the box. How far can you sustain the strong shape of the body?

Repeat these ideas in twos or threes so that the space and forcefulness is shared.

In twos, explore cooperative strength and opposing strength.

lifting a box

pushing a load

giving and taking a rope, a cooperative tug-of-war

a work action as in sawing or rowing

rising and sinking together or in opposition

towards and away, matching or opposite

In twos throw and catch light airflow balls. Repeat as if the ball were very heavy, repeat without the ball and in bigger groups. Imagine that the ball is explosive, wet, sticky, smelly, alive ...

Pick up, carry and place a chair very carefully, repeat as if it were much heavier, repeat without using the chair.

Pick up, carry and place imaginary objects: baskets, logs, sacks, packing-cases; repeat in twos or larger groups.

This activity can also make use of gym mats which is an interesting way for the children to learn how to get them out, then use the mats as a magic carpet for story-telling (see also Lesson 8).

Development

Work actions and carrying actions using strength; extend the group size, combine the whole class; add rhythm and phrase using percussion and voice; add travel and changes of level, real or imaginary; add a context such as slaves rowing, mechanical motion that breaks down, refugees carrying all their belongings, pioneers, a journey through thick undergrowth/mud/water/snow.

Lesson 15: Opposition; Action and Reaction; A Dance Fight (8–13)

This is a tightly controlled and choreographed sequence. It makes use of balance, movement control, and memory.

Begin with making statues to illustrate actions such as punching, jabbing, poking, pushing, kicking, swiping, butting, batting.

Join some of these movements together in slow motion. Have plenty of space and be aware of other people's movements. Use a variety of body parts to change the action and the shape of the body, and exaggerate the shape and size.

kick   shove   jab   butt

Discover the body shapes that might have received these actions: duck, flinch, fall, spin, recoil, cower, cover. Try movements in slow motion, exaggerate to emphasize the body shape.

recoil   flinch   fall   duck

Work with a partner again using space so that there is no body contact. Select a sequence of about four moves to make a slow motion fight. Alternate so that the attacker is then attacked and recovery becomes preparation. Incorporate travel and change of level. All movements must be absolutely controlled and the sequence repeated accurately.

i   *ii*   *iii*   *iv*

Choreograph all the class sequences so that they follow with no gaps. This requires very accurate timing and well rehearsed sequences. Repeat at speed for fun!

Weightlessness

Lesson 16: Sensing Lightness (6−7)

Classical ballet is an example of how much energy and control is required to lift the body against the downward heavy pull of gravity. Although this weightlessness contrasts with body weight and forceful movement it must not be confused with giving in to the gravitational pull which becomes heaviness and the body may sufficiently relax to collapse completely.

The quality of weightlessness is often more difficult to find than force. It is as much an attitude as a technique and needs concentration. Concrete and imaginary images of weightlessness contribute to this attitude.

Blow some bubbles and watch as they lift, float, settle and disappear. Use arms, hands, and the whole body in a similar way.

Watch the way a blown-up balloon settles on the ground and gently wobbles. Try the same movement with the whole body; vary the shape and body support.

Watch small feathers, down or tufts of cottonwool. Blow them into the air. Keep them up, then watch the pathway of the particle as it floats down.

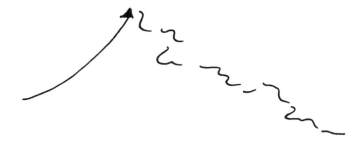

Blow your own hand gently as if it were such a feather; imitate the pathway. Add the body to the hand, using different parts of the body to lead upwards and to lead downwards.

Create a phrase of movement using sudden lightness, then a wandering pathway to settle slowly on the floor.

Repeat the sequence three times, increasing the length of time. How slowly and lightly can you settle while still moving all the time?

Watch a partner's sequence. Find words or sounds to describe the movement. Quietly utter the words or sounds to accompany your partner's movement.

Join the two sequences together and accompany your own movement.

Lesson 17: Developing a Phrase of Light Movement (7– 8)

Working in twos, one is passive, one leads. Arrange partner's arms, head, back, as if creating a sculpture. Work as if the partner is very fragile, take great care of the person and understand the structure of the body so that all positions are very comfortable.

Change role, create given images to illustrate words or characters: frost, wilderness, mist, labour, protective, searching.

Lead partner around the space with the lightest handhold. Partner could close eyes, but must feel safe.

One partner manages two or three others, placing and arranging the bodies. Create a sequence: lead A..........
lead B ....
lead C ....
lead A ....
lead B .... retain the sense
of lightness and non-disturbance.

In twos, with the lightest touch, motivate your partner who responds, alternate this touch and response, vary the movement ... part, follow, turn, lean, travel, sink, lift and pause.

123

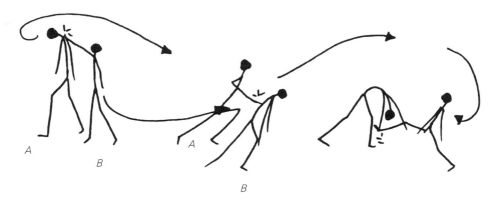

Stand still in larger groups, one person moves around the group, who move very slightly as the mover passes.

In a group, suggest a disturbance that passes through, repeat but accentuate the beginning/end/middle.

Give more force to the accent, gradually decreasing weight into lightness. Find appropriate group shapes to create a logical sequence: coming together ... fracture ... fragment ... disperse ... assemble elsewhere.

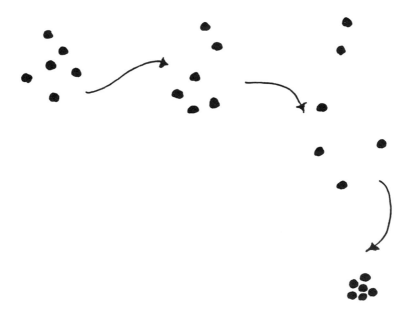

Lesson 18: Weight and Rhythm (Any Age)

Stepping and clapping
Stamp and jump with force, use the sound of the feet, make your feet louder than anyone else's! Stamp the feet as if crushing insects/nuts/beans. Change

direction, play with different size steps: as small as possible, as huge as possible.

Alternate stamping with absolute stillness and silence, either self-directed or directed by the teacher's tambour.

Create a pattern in time to the tambour: [o = rest]

|– – – – | o o o o | – – – – – | o o o o | – – – – |

Alternate with a partner, or alternate half a class with the other half.

A. | – – – – | o o o o | – – – – |

B. | o o o o | – – – – | o o o o |

Travel with even steps, stamp each step.
Stamp only with the same foot, 1 2 /1 2 /1 2 /1 2 / (2/4 time).

Stamp on alternate feet using three counts,
1 2 3 /1 2 3 /1 2 3 / (3/4 time).

Accompany steps with clapping, alternate claps and stamps. Try clapping twice to one step, clapping on the first beat of 3/4 time and so on.

Development
Stamp or clap at the beginning of a movement, allow the movement to fade away until nothing is left. Change the level and placing of each movement.

Create a sequence of four movements, practice and repeat them. Adjust the sequence to fit a regular sound rhythm;

Dance the sequence with a partner: copy exactly; contrast; alternate; or combine the individual movements.

Vary the rhythmic pattern, increase or decrease the speed, change the bar length:

/- //- - //- - - //- - - - //- - - - - //

Reverse the pattern and add the two together:

/- //- - //- - - //- - - - //- - - //- - //- //

Add percussion and/or voice.

Lines and Structure; Dimensions

Introduction

Straight lines are fundamentally more to do with the sense of sight than with bodily movement and frequently occur in young childrens's drawing. Straight lines are difficult to produce in dance since arms and legs, fingers and hands are levers which when moved make curved pathways.

> The straight line introduces linear extension in space and thereby the notion of direction. In keeping with the law of differentiation, the first relation between directions to be acquired is the simplest one, that of the right angle. The rightangular crossing stands for all angular relations until obliqueness is explicitly mastered and differentiated from rightangularity. The right angle is the simplest because it creates a symmetrical pattern, and it is the basis for the framework of vertical and horizontal, on which rests our entire conception of space.
>
> (Arnheim, 1974)

The vertical line in bodily movement is introduced by gravitational pull, and the horizontal line by the bilateral structure of the body, which reaches across or away from the vertical line of the body.

We know about rising and sinking, about gravitational pull, about balance, location and spatial orientation by living in the physical world, by seeing it and bodily feeling it. The flatness of the floor, the uprightness of walls and the lines of structure that we continually see around us, enable us to balance and to place ourselves, to relate to the environment, and to organize our behaviour. The concepts of verticality and of horizontality are dependent on both visual and kinesthetic sensing.

The notion of verticality

Up / down / standing / gravity / rising / sinking / support / pole / mast / stem / growth / elongated / climb / steep / elevate / stature / towards heaven / infinity / towards the floor / earth / stability.

Sensing the verticality of the body introduces good posture and accurate alignment of the body, which is more likely to need remedial help in adults than in young children. Good posture allows the body to move with the least amount of stress and combats the gravitational pull of the body towards the earth centre; body parts that are out of line react to gravity adversely.

Balance

The body is relatively unstable in a standing position, the most stable position being aligned over the base support. The closer the body centre of gravity to the centre of its base support, the more balanced the body. Posture positioning is controlled by visual cues, by the inner ear, and by receptors in tendons, joints, and muscles.

The plumb line should run evenly down the entire length of the body.

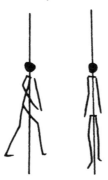

When the accurate centre line of the body is felt, there is a sense of weightlessness that seems to lift the body out of its gravitational dependency, it is about 'thinking tall', with its upward release of energy, in contrast to the downward absence of energy that accompanies fatigue and depression.

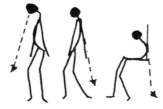

The concept of verticality is continually reinforced by visual experience. Note especially the square lines in Western architecture, observe the shape of the classroom, note the walls, ceiling, windows and doors, street planning, and so on.

Lesson 19: Horizontality (7+)

Make body shapes that are associated with flat, floor, surface, lying down, horizon, across, strata, sedimentary, layer.

The awareness of horizontality is most easily established by lying on the floor and being aware of the level surface. This includes bodily contact with a flat surface and the shape and feel of body weight.

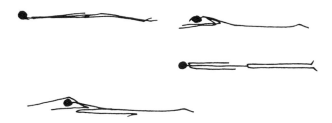

Visual awareness: notice the floor surface when lying, sitting, and standing. Notice the horizontal structure of the room/hall, ceiling meets wall, beams, tops of windows, and doors. Notice parallel lines and constancy of shape and the effect of the viewpoint. On the glass of large window, trace and draw the flat lines in the view; find out about projection.

Use the body to find lines of horizontality, accepting the necessary lines of support.

Use each other and objects, such as chairs and stage blocks to achieve really flat lines.

Without the support, select three or four of these shapes and join them together to make a sequence, either retaining or breaking the line. Use the sequence to travel. Remember that the hands and feet are extensions of the legs and arm, and the head an extension of the spine. Feel the energy going beyond the limit of the body.

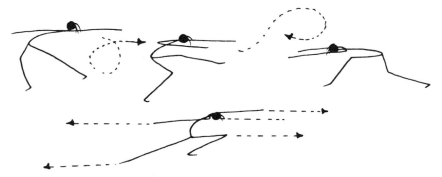

In twos or small groups combine these individual sequences so that the horizontal lines are shared and joined.

Develop a motif; repeat it changing the level and the front, add travel across the space to emphasize the 'horizon'.

Each dancer learn all the motifs within the group and perform these motifs in unison or in canon.

Consider the context of the performance. The sequence could be about landscape, water, sky, tranquillity, or peace.

Visual horizontality

The horizon is at eye level no matter where the level of the eyes. Make drawings from a variety of eye levels: the floor; sitting; standing on a table. This reinforces the notion of horizontality and encourages the consideration of different viewpoints.

The artist Mondrian reduced his conception of the world to the dynamic relationship between verticality as the line of aspiration and horizontality as the line of stability.

Lesson 20: Verticality (7+)

Use the body to explore vertical lines (in the classroom as part of an art or maths lesson).

Stand in parallel groups, parallel to the wall.

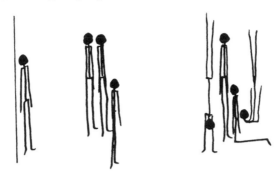

Find postures that combine horizontal and vertical lines and notice the angles thus formed.

Create shapes in twos and threes in which these lines cross, overlap, extend, match, and contrast.

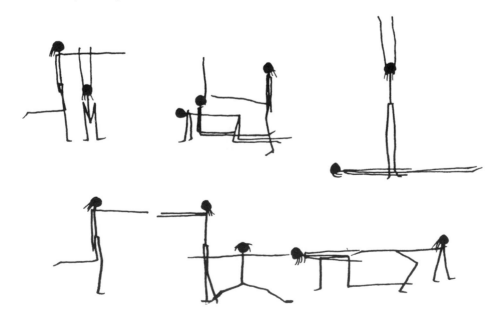

Using a skeleton or each other, find body parts that can bend or make curves such as fingers, hands, arms, and spine. Investigate the skeletal frame of the body.

Imagine (or create!) a classroom in which the objects are out of alignment; notice how we hang pictures straight. Try hanging pictures, art work and notices crooked ... what is the effect? Why is it difficult to work on a table with uneven legs, or to sit on a tilted chair? Why can horses sleep standing up? What is the difference between things that stand on one, two, three, and four legs?

Explore leaning lines and leaning bodies. How do they look and feel?

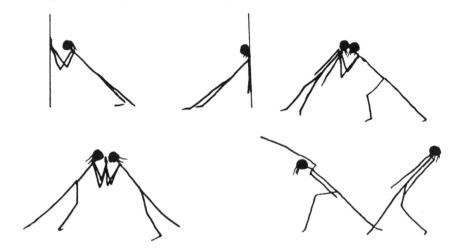

Explore broken straight lines, use bent straws for reference.

Create a movement motif in which the body line becomes increasingly broken.

Explore the mood, feeling and meaning of this sequence. Consider movements that snap, break, rupture, fracture, are riven and torn.

Change the speed and the continuity using jerky, sudden, gradual, smooth, continuous and interrupted movements.

Combine several bodies to create a group motif. Consider the effect of overlapping in front or behind; moving in unison; moving one at a time; identical shapes; joined shapes.

Choreograph a motif with six bodies incorporating four changes of shape: reach, lean, snap, fold. Reverse the sequence and use words or rhythm music.

The motif could be used in a dance study about landscape; disintegration; earthquake; collapse; assembling; construction and destruction.

Lesson 21: Inside and Outside — Looking at Fruit (7+)

This lesson deals with inside and outside and the notion of protection, with reference to the flesh around the stone of a fruit such as a plum or cherry.

Wrap a fruit for each child in several layers of soft paper, possibly enclosed in a box. Each child unwraps the package secretly and carefully. During this process the children may be instructed to 'freeze' to note shapes of hands, body and place of focus.

Break or bite the fruit. Note the flesh surrounding the stone. Investigate kinds of fruit (e.g. coconut, orange, strawberry) and their different means of protecting the seed.

Dance

Using individual movement, be aware of the softer parts of the body: the under surface of the arms, under the chin, the chest and the stomach. Note and perform gestures and posture associated with fear in which the soft parts are protected, the body drawing in around the body centre.

Explore folding inwards by bringing the left to the right and the right to the left ... gather in, huddle, withdraw, shrink from, hide. Change the body weight and use twisting with isolated or whole bodily movement. Repeat the movement ideas as big/as small as possible.

Watch people's gestures, and interpret them. Can you recognize lack of confidence, fear, privacy, being cold or shy?

Find out about the formation of fruit from flowering to ripening.

Consider the dispersal of seeds ... the dandelion clock, ash keys, willow-herb parachutes, lupins which twist to eject the seed.

Explore unfolding / opening / exploding / jubilation / extending / scattering / opening away from the body centre, taking the right to the right and the left to the left to reveal the body centre. Emphasize one side of the body using the other to echo the movement.

It may be necessary to work on technique here such as relaxed shoulders rotation of the arm and leg to facilitate this open feeling. Explore asymmetry, change of level or focus, turning, and change of direction.

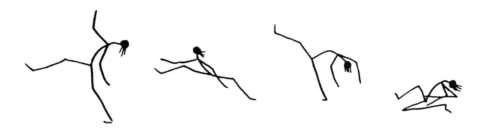

Add closing-in movement to opening movement. Explore the mood and feeling. Closing in centres on the self and privacy, whereas opening out is public and embraces the outside world. Find dynamic qualities to emphasize these feelings such as:

gathering slowly ..... withdraw/stand off,
gathering quickly ..... flinch/rebuff,
open suddenly ..... excitement/joy,
open slowly ..... hope/revelation.

Create a motif 'sandwich':

Open/close/open. Close/open/close.
Refine and practice.
Repeat three times, increasing the size.

Create a group dance to show the growth and the formation of a shape that contains, and a shape that is contained.

Open up the shapes to release space and energy outward.

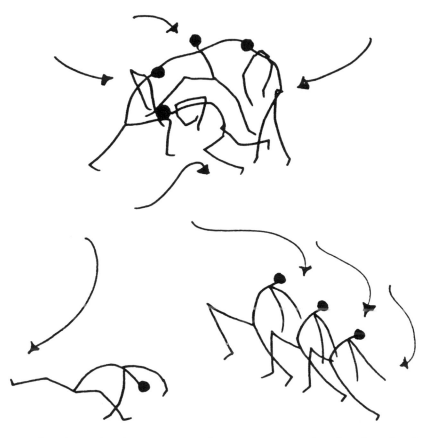

Repeat the dance in the reverse order to express a barrier; imprisoning; trapping. Review and refine any changes in dynamics and shaping.

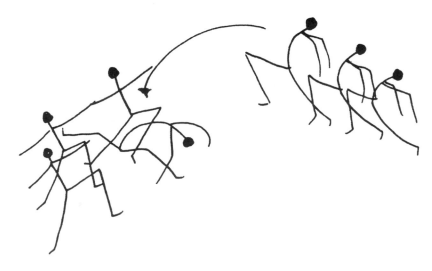

Duo dance

Individually explore the shape of the body as a container. Create holes and spaces, sides and openings.

Individually explore the body shape as if it were contained in a confined space. Vary the weight support and the shape.

In twos, combine these two ideas.

Make a sequence to alternate the roles. Consider the transitions using change of speed, place, force, and level, to create a logical and continuous study.

Consider the effect of removing the 'contained' body. Does the container collapse, wait, or change?

Consider the effect of removing the container. Does the protected body become exposed, disintegrate, perish, grow in strength and become independent, or flee?

Discuss the difference between protection and imprisonment; between being sheltered and confined; and the interdependence between those who protect and those who are protected.

Create a group dance and perform it as an expression of captivity and then as an expression of caring. Observe, note and refine changes in the movement and structure.

Further development
Investigate shells and shellfish; packaging; three-dimensional structure and design, building up models and carving out spaces.

Lesson 22: Inside and Outside — Looking at an Onion (7+)

Cut in half an onion, draw and note its structure.

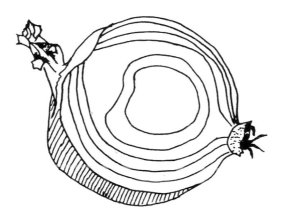

Separate each layer, noting the shape and relationship of each successive layer. Consider the notion of parallel lines in the curves. Compare the centre with the external layer, investigate old and new onions and stages of growth.
Draw, label, describe.

Dance
Each child is one layer and finds a layer shape and a way of becoming that shape. Add individual layer shapes to create a cross-section. Consider transitions and ways of moving into place.

Create a group dance, increasing the number of bodies to make outer layers. Consider stages of wrapping and explore the qualities of protection, encircling, and wrapping around. Reflect these qualities in the shape of the body and in the movement.
Reverse the process to combine wrapping and unwrapping.

wrapping

unwrapping

Action

Lesson 23: The Way Animals Move; The Snail (6–13)

Observe the way animals move by watching animals in the classroom, such as fish, tadpoles, hamsters, mice, snails, stick insects, minibeasts, spiders.

Discuss the movements, exploring words. For example, find words that describe the way a snail moves: slow, pushing, squeezing, sluggish, sliding, leisurely, successive, smooth, immobile, languid, gradual, emerging, withdrawing, gradual, imperceptible.

Compare different animal movements, trying to be as accurate as possible. Do animals of the same kind move in the same way?

Record an animal's movement using video / words / photographs / drawings / notation.

Movement

It is important to realise that DANCE IS NOT ABOUT CHILDREN BEING ANIMALS, but is about children observing movement to extend their own movement vocabulary. A dance about snails is a dance using human dance movement to explore snail-like qualities.

Using the observation of a snail, practise some of the movements with the hands only, with the feet, the head and the whole body. Consider which bit moves first and where, explore essential elements such as carrying a shell, maintaining contact with the surface, slowness.

Shape a snail in clay, draw a snail, write a poem describing a snail.

Find out about the life of a snail, about different species and habitats, about food, life span, shell markings, reproduction.

Create snail-like images in music, dance, poetry, three-dimensional and two-dimensional art, using information and observation to clarify the form. This approach will help the children embody the snail-like qualities in their art work.

As an experiment you may like to compare the work based on first-hand experience with text-book information.

There are many opportunities for close observation and analysis in and out of school, for example, birds in the playground; microscopes and minibeasts; an aquarium; creatures seen on farm and zoo visits; animals brought to school such as pet rabbits. The above snail example can apply generally.

Development

Investigate the movement behaviour of creatures when sleeping, when afraid, or when feeding, and use sequences of such movement ideas to create dance studies.

The observation of real creatures is also a sound basis for creating imaginary animals, and for the understanding of animal metaphors in language and story.

Lesson 24: Looking at Plants: 'Once upon a time there was a forest'. (Any Age)

Imagine the dense growth of different trees and plants and the relationship between them. Base the movement study on real examples to clarify the movement and to develop observation and interest.

Example 1

The king of the forest: huge oak trees can measure 40 feet round and there are some growing in this country over 600 years old.

Movement

Consider posture and stand with a very strong base; feel wide and tall and imagine cushions of space under the arms held to form part of the trunk. Use deep slow breathing and concentrate on the feeling of stability. Imagine the roots below you and the branches above and the history you might have witnessed.

Can you move into and out of these positions with a feeling of age and strength?

Example 2

Trees that weep and tremble such as willow and poplar trees. Look at weeping willows. What gives them their hanging appearance? Hang crêpe paper streamers and watch how they move as you walk past or make a draught.

Movement

Which body parts can hang? Can you move as if they are lightly suspended?

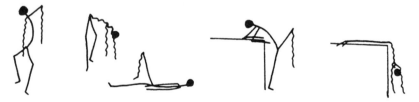

Use paper streamers to emphasize the shape and movement.

Investigate the effect of the wind on plants. The long stalks which are flattened sideways explain the almost ceaseless movement of aspen trees. Try trembling movements using hands and fingers, arms, torso, and whole body.

Assemble groups that tremble and sway, move as the wind disturbs the group from, say, high to low or back to front.

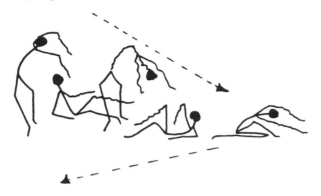

Example 3

Plants and trees with thorns and prickles: holly and blackthorn.

In the past holly trees survived because superstition associated them with the power to ward off evil.

Blackthorn, in unapproachable thickets, gives protection to other plants growing underneath and to nesting birds by warding off people and grazing animals.

Observe and draw holly leaves and the thorny twigs of blackthorn.

Figure 19   Observing prickles and thorns in the classroom. Using hands to explore shapes with as many points as possible.

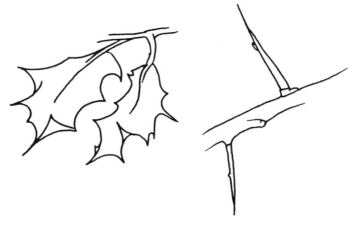

Movement

How many body parts can be pointed? Make shapes with as many points as possible.

Find ways of getting into and out of these shapes that look sharp and damaging: prod, poke, jab, stab, prick, sting.

Use words or voice sounds to accompany the movements.

Example 4

Plants that climb and wind: ivy and columbine.

Observe and compare the way these plants are supported using suckers, tendrils and spiral stems. Investigate parasitic plants such as dodder, toothwort, and mistletoe.

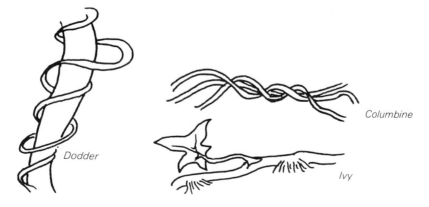

Dodder

Columbine

Ivy

Movement
Use arms, head and spine to make winding spiral movements. Use these movements to travel and grow in size. Wind the body around a chair or around each other.

Wind through spaces made by groups of bodies.

Example 5
Fallen trees, broken branches, decay.
Combine these movements to create a forest. Individuals and groups contribute one or several examples.
Consider related shapes. Who moves first, when, and where?

Development
Possible contexts could include stories such as 'The Sleeping Beauty' or 'The Brave Little Tailor'. Plant and environmental studies. Growth and structure.

Lesson 25: Looking at Ball Games — Stepping Actions and Gestures (7–13)

The starting point is a ball game: pig in the middle. The development of the lesson could be taken from any game.
Play and observe. Use airflow balls or rolled-up socks and play a real game. Play for long enough for the children to feel competitive and sufficiently motivated to want to get the ball. Some catching and throwing ability helps!
The class observes one or two games and notes the bodily actions: leaping turning, stepping, reaching, dodging, running, hopping, skipping, as well as throwing and catching.
Repeat the game without the ball at natural speed and in slow motion.

Working individually, extract some of these movements to make a sequence. With the help of a partner, refine and perform this sequence.

Learn a partner's sequence, join the two together and perform in unison.

In groups of four, use the two duos to compose a study. Consider unison and alternation.

Refer to dance compositional forms and compose a class study. This might include:

Unison: all perform one sequence.

Question and answer: A, B, then A, then B.

Canon: individual or group studies as a round (three groups are sufficient as more are difficult to follow.)

Rondo: use a sequence as chorus; each 'verse' is performed by one group while others remain still. This requires accurate timing.

Development

Create a sound accompaniment.

Modify the class dance to fit a piece of recorded music. A simple and continous rhythm is essential: Scott Joplin's music would be suitable.

143

Mary Lowden

Language, Voice and Movement

Lesson 26: Body Percussion and Speech Sounds (Any Age)

Explore body percussive sounds; clap hands; clap body sides; clap the floor. Make the sound loud; soft; fast; slow; intermittent; rhythmic.

Clap to accompany self or partner walking, running, and stopping.

Repeat with fingers tapping or clicking. Combine claps and clicking.

Explore humming. Consider pitch; volume; continuity; harmony; place of sound if the class is dispersed; number of people humming.

Move and hum to find appropriate accompaniment, and use the breath to phrase the movement and sound.

Explore mouth sounds such as plop; squelch; squeak; suck; kiss; shshsh; lalala; click; tuttut; hiss; rrrrr;

Select three sounds and three movements to make a sequence, using repetition. Find a way to start and finish.

Development

Make a group sequence combining words and sounds for another group or individual to match with a movement sequence and visual score.
For example:

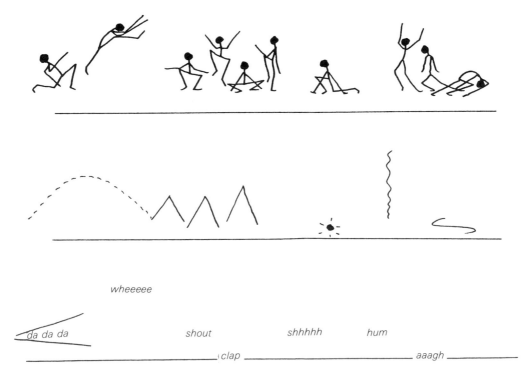

144

Reverse the sequence. Make a sequence that is as contrasting as possible.

Start with a common 'score'. Work separately on the sound and movement. Combine the two ... without changing the initial composition unless that is the intention.

Lesson 27: Voice Accompaniment; Using Names (Any Age)

The use of the voice to accompany movement is difficult and introductory work must use ideas and vocabulary that are both clear and familiar; a touch of humour will help if the work appears too simple and obvious!

Using names
Start near the floor and practice 'jack-in-the-box' jumps. Move as fast and high as possible. Try three jumps in a row to a given drum beat. Without the drum, repeat the three jumps, adding pauses. With a starting jump as a cue, the whole class perform the three jumps. This is effective if spread over some time. Develop adding more jumps and planned order.

The same class sit and call out their names. The name is added to the jump(s). Make it sharp and in time. Use the spoken name to rise slowly; get up with jerky staccato movements.

movements; get down as if melting or collapsing. How would you say the name for these movements?

Select a pattern of three movements and matching name sounds.

Development
Perform individual pattern within a small group and choreograph to add order or context.

145

Voice and movement description

Walk around the space saying 'walk' for each step. Repeat but change to running; hopping; jumping. Vary the speed, volume, pitch, duration, and timbre to match voice and movement.

Repeat using the voice to make a running commentary instead of separate words.

For example:

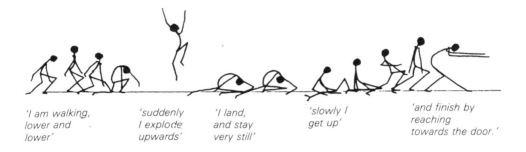

'I am walking, lower and lower'

'suddenly I explode upwards'

'I land, and stay very still'

'slowly I get up'

'and finish by reaching towards the door.'

Development

Repeat the idea of a commentary to express possible feelings or situations.

For example:

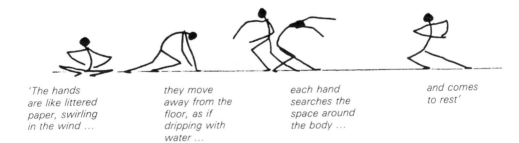

'The hands are like littered paper, swirling in the wind ...

they move away from the floor, as if dripping with water ...

each hand searches the space around the body ...

and comes to rest'

In twos, make commentary to accompany the partner's movement; change role maintaining continuity. This work should be spontaneous and explorative; some ideas will not work, while others may stimulate discussion and practice. Partners can be supportive or challenging according to the level of confidence and imagination. Quiet speaking affords necessary privacy and control.

Development

Using poetry, see Lessons 29 and 30 and read the preceding introduction.

Lesson 28: Words and Meaning in Movement; Opposites (8+)

Introductory movement work
Explore change in body weight support, body shape and managed transitions using body parts to lead specific movements, with reference to deep and high and body awareness.

Using a pair of balance scales
Observe the movement of the pans in a pair of balance scales. Increase and decrease the weighed materials so that the scales move very slowly, and quicker, and attain absolute balance.

Discuss difference and similarity in the weight. Discuss difference and similarity in feelings, or situations: like/hate, gloomy/light, freedom/captivity, strong/weak, lost/found, disappointment/anticipation.

Using the scales as an illustration, discuss the relationship between opposites ... compromise, opposition, alternation, neutrality.

Using movement and working in twos, take up a high and low position, change shapes.

Swop places, stopping at the position of equality. Break down the transition into five locations, the third being absolutely equal.

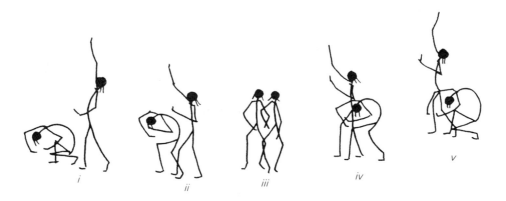

Develop the starting shapes to express opposite feelings or situations.
For example:

> Smooth ....Jagged.

> Benevolent ....Merciless.

This requires concentration and the sharing of experience and understanding to really tease out the meanings. (Some adults find this more difficult than children, not trusting their 'hunches' or kinesthetic information.)

Identify the transition between the meanings of the words, including the neutral state. Find words and phrases to describe or name the starting place and the transition, and use words to accompany every movement., the same for each dancer but in opposite order. Refine and edit, omitting any superfluous words or movements.

This will take time. Allow opportunity for discussion, practice, and investigation in a class lesson. Do not be tempted to direct or provide material, but share in the discussion or question if necessary. The process of exploring and discovering language and meaning is vital.

Similar exercise

In small groups, illustrate three given words that are close or opposite in meaning using three still movement groups. Decide on the order of words and add transitional movements to join the three group shapes together. This will involve investigation of meaning, related significance and the notion of cause and effect.

Some examples of word groups are:

> Horror .... Sinister ...... Safe
> Anxious .... Disturbed ...... Tranquil
> Delicate ..... Lifeless .... Vigorous

Development

Children select words for themselves or each other. Read poems that express similar ideas.

In a class of differing ethnic language, compare sound and words of similar meaning.

Art work: explore opposite and similar colours; consider harmony, contrast, opposition, merging, complementing. Using modelling or sculpture materials, create forms that express ideas used in the dance studies; can transition be shown in a fixed form? Consider texture and materials.

Look at the work of sculptors. Do titles help?

Using Poetry — An Introduction

The commentary idea suggested in Lesson 27 can be developed so that lines of poetry prompt ideas and feelings in movement as well as the reading and understanding of poetry. Poetry must be selected with movement in mind, and the movement should capture the feel and form of the poem. The phrasing of each statement is important, as is the style and mood. Some poems also set a rhythm, for example T.S. Eliot's 'Railway Cat', which could accompany railway station actions and events.

Start with short selected poetry passages and allow time for understanding, exploration and refinement, rather than working through several lines or verses. There may well be as many interpretations as children in the class, so that teaching is individual and learning is about sharing ideas.

Begin the lesson with some appropriate movement to establish the atmosphere and possible movement vocabulary. Once the poem is introduced such introductory work is an intrusion.

Lesson 29: Poetry — 'Mushrooms' by Sylvia Plath (10+)

Overnight, very
Whitely, discreetly,
Very quietly

Our toes, our noses
Take hold on the loam,
Acquire the air.

Nobody sees us,
Stops us, betrays us;
The small grains make room.

Soft fists insist on
Heaving the needles,
The leafy bedding,

Even the paving.
Our hammers, our rams,
Earless and eyeless,

Perfectly voiceless,
Widen the crannies,
Shoulder through holes. We

Diet on water,
On crumbs of shadow,
Bland-mannered, asking

Little or nothing.
So many of us!
So many of us!

We are shelves, we are
Tables, we are meek,
We are edible,

Nudgers and shovers
In spite of ourselves.
Our kind multiplies:

We shall by morning
Inherit the earth.
Our foot's in the door.

Consider the poem and identify its content, mood and style. Identify related movement ideas.

As an introductory movement, work on horizontal shapes and actions. In sitting, lying and standing positions, explore flat step-like movements that take you from one level to the next. Use the hands, and be very precise.

Use chairs, tables, stage blocks to build a structure of horizontal planes. Use the movement of the hands and body to move on and beside this structure considering the mood of the poem and the feel/look of mushrooms. Make step-like movements that get higher in separate moves. Develop and edit the structure and the movement of the group to suggest a community appearing in silence. Each choose a starting level that is generally hidden.

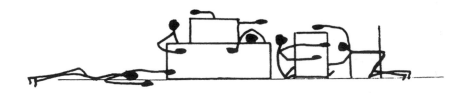

Using a copy of the whole poem, select a line or word or phrase and repeat it to accompany your own individual movement. You must move and speak but may do neither separately; when not moving the body must be absolutely still. Arrange the movement and speech passages to begin according to the order in the text; accept omissions and doubling and overlapping.

Run the sequence through, refine and modify if necessary.

Lesson 30: Poetry — 'Water Picture' by Mary Swenson (8+)

Water Picture

In the pond in the park
all things are doubled:
Long buildings hang and
wriggle gently. Chimneys
are bent legs bouncing
on clouds below. A flag
wags like a fishhook
down there in the sky.

Introductory movement

Explore the possible shapes and movements made with the arms and hands. Consider: symmetry; leading and following; line; near and far. Consider: turn; wave; flutter; hang; loose; stiff; rigid. Add some of these movements together, each having the same length of time, add pauses. Emphasize the line with the rest of the body and stepping.

Listen to the poem, listen again and respond with movement. Select some of the movements and develop them.

Work in groups of four. Each remember a line of the poem. Speak and move for each other considering the movements and the relationship between the group members as they move. Join the phrases of movement together including any repetition, and speak the words to create a dance poem.

Development

Work with a second group to explore the idea of reflection and mirroring.

Use an overhead projector to throw up broken images on the dancers or back screen.

Relationship

Lesson 31: Working with Objects: Stage Blocks (8–13)

As in language, meaning in dance is in the relationship between any elements in the dance, between dancer and dancer, dancer and space, space and audience, one movement and another, movement and music, and so on. Meaning is discovered through making dance, watching dance, and exploring ideas through movement as well as of movement. The following suggestions are additional objective exercises to develop an awareness of the significance of relationship in dance.

In this activity, objectivity is emphasized by using stage blocks, although chairs and other classroom furniture could be used instead. Ideally each dancer has a stage block that will support the weight of the body. Large blocks of staging can be shared as long as the task is solved individually.

Using a block, improvise to find ways in which a still body shape can express the following relationships with the block: oppose, dominate, support, be supported, worship, cherish, extend, possess, be possessed, surround, trap, be trapped, threaten, be threatened, protect, be protected, destroy, be destroyed.

Consider the difference between real actions and the dance image. Although you cannot actually support a large block you can relate to the block as if to give it support. Use the shape of the body, point of contact, focus and placing of body parts rather than mimed actions, omitting facial and gestural expressions.

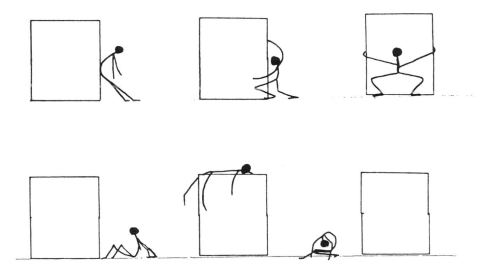

Are there some ideas that are easier than others? Are some ideas immediate while others need thinking about? Show and compare other interpretations in the class; discuss.

View the studies from different angles and make small changes to explore the effect on the meaning.

Select one idea, and find ways of getting into the position without changing the meaning. Omit any irrelevant or unnecessary movements. Consider starting place, direction and approach; speed; action; phrasing. Use a partner as spectator and 'reader', and select the most significant movements. Why are they significant?

Observe two different interpretations of the same meaning and discuss.

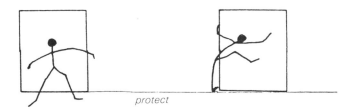

protect

Are there differences between how a movement feels in performance and how it looks to a spectator?

Repeat the activity but find ways of moving out of the position. Join together the approach, the position and the departure.

Development

Repeat this sequence but with a change of meaning; show and discuss.

Work in a similar way with an empty space, and with an object. Try working objectively with another dancer. How difficult is it to omit subjective feeling? Why?

Work in groups to explore the possible relationship and change of relationship between groups or between a group and an individual.

Consider the relationship, music and movement. Using a familiar place of music make a dance accompaniment that (i) reflects the music; (ii) is in opposition to the music; (iii) is as if trying to escape from the music.

153

Lesson 32: Focus — Using the Eyes (6–13)

How and where a dancer looks plays a crucial role in what is being communicated and whether it matters. The eyes are a giveaway, not because the dancer must look where he is going, but because the eyes clearly show, even from a distance, the level of commitment and the feel of the dance. Watching a dancer whose eyes are not part of the movement is like talking to someone whose gaze is elsewhere. Young children find it easier than adults to be wholly involved in an activity, and this includes their eyes, but as part of their understanding of dance they need to be aware of the effect of focus.

Eyes establish a relationship with places, objects and people, as well as audience, and relationship gives meaning. Eyes can also imply a relationship with something imagined thus giving a meaning to an empty space.

Sitting together, watch as a child or teacher walks around the class, following the pathway closely. Take it in turns to walk and feel what it is like to be watched.

Watch an imaginary walker. How can you give the impression that everyone is watching the same person? Do you need to plan, fix cues or nominate leaders?

Watch an imaginary spider, or any other creature, whose pathway is described by the teacher. Perhaps the creature climbs walls and crosses the ceiling or goes in and out of closed windows.

Add the slightest movement possible to emphasize your focus as if you are watching with the body as well.

Add movements that show your response, which may be curiosity or fear, so that you need to look more closely or stand back.

Always keep a space so that a spectator has a view of the relationship, and can feel the tension between the object and subject.

Work with a partner and move separately around the space, but maintain eye contact. Retreat and advance to discover the most powerful distance and contact, create a tension between you and hold it as you change level or distance.

Watch your hands as one moves apart. What is the difference in feeling between focusing on the stationary hand, the moving hand, or the destination?

Work in threes or fours, changing the relationship by changing the focus. It there opposition? Rejection of one? Equality?

As a group, establish a common bond and relate to an imagined object on the floor. Using focus, explore the relationship with the object, consider distance and any boundary around the object. Using focus, retain the relationship but change the nature or place of the object — the object may fly, explode, disappear, or divide. Discuss and develop or try another idea.

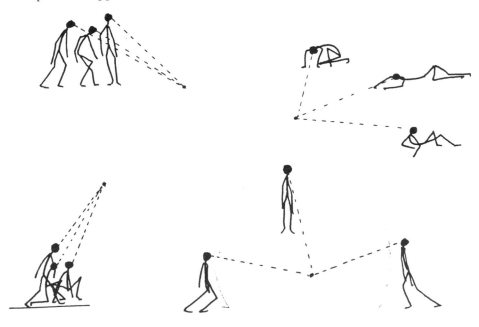

Lesson 33: Focus and Context (8–13)

Individually focus on objects around you, look and move the head towards the object getting as near as possible while remaining on the spot, change the object of focus and explore changes in body shape using turns and twists and different levels.

In a small group, move individually towards a focus using others as obstacles to be climbed over or crawled through with as little deviation in line as possible (see also Lesson 12).

Change focus to recross the group and add gestures to suggest a need such as hunger or escape. What is the possible context?

Create a group sequence in which individual focus becomes a group focus. What is the motivation? How is this expressed in the transitional movements?

Explore possible contexts such as searching for a rare butterfly; avoiding danger; the arrival of an important person; suspecting a spy; meeting something from another world. Retain the object of focus as imaginary, and add a happening or story which is stated by the focusing. Discuss, plan and develop the study with the help of a spectator group so that the sequence is clear and logical.

Development

Group focus can be used to imply an event or activity in dance-drama performances, for example:

The passing of carts to collect the dead in a dance-drama about the great plague.

The first aeroplane flight.

The fight between David and Goliath.

The arrival of the bad fairy in 'The Sleeping Beauty.'

The story of 'The Emperor's New Clothes'.

Music and Dance

Lesson 34: Using Classroom Instruments (5–13)

Exploring the quality of sound and movement accompaniment

The following exercises are introductory and provide preparatory work for sound accompaniment suggested in many of the lesson examples. Making sound requires sensitive movement and very careful listening. A long session might ask too much of a young child's concentration. A little and often is more appropriate in the infant school.

According to experience, instruments are played by the teacher, by a music group, or by the dance class. Encourage listening skills by focusing on one particular instrument or kind of sound.

Example 1: The cymbal

Listen to one strike of the cymbal and the duration of the sound. Is this different near or further away? Touch the cymbal and feel the vibrations. Find out about sound waves. Make *one* movement to last as long as the sound and even imagine it lasting longer.

Accent, Impulse

Listen as the cymbal is struck hard and the sound fades, repeat the single movement with decreasing speed/size/force/height/, using all or some of these dynamic qualities.

Accent, Impact

Listen as the cymbal is played continuously with an increase in sound. Match this sound with a movement that increases in its dynamic qualities.

Add the two sounds and the two movements together to make a sequence with the accent in the middle or at the beginning and end.

Perform this kind of movement as a group; try increasing and decreasing the number of dancers.

Example 2: Shaker, maracca

Turn the shaker slowly, pause and repeat. How small a sound can be made or heard? Make a movement that is equally small or tiny. Try rolling, stepping or changing the shape of the body. Make each move holding a shaker. Can you move so that the shaker makes a small sound? Add pauses and stillness. Listen and watch as a group move: can the sound and the movement travel through the class as a slight wind disturbs reeds or dead leaves?

Listen to the sound of the wind. Explore other sounds that can only just be heard and consider accompanying movement.

Example 3: Drum (see also Lesson 18)

Listen to the sound of the beater as it strikes the different surfaces of the drum and make steps to match. Use different parts of the feet and play with strong spaced-out steps or quick tiny steps.

Alternate these steps and sounds to make a thythmic pattern.

Add change of direction, change of dancer, speed, level, etc.

Rhythm is a combination of weight and time. Stamp to a drum beat with equal accent and even time.

Accent one foot,

Accent alternate feet,

beat the drum and walk with an even pulse.

Think of the steps in groups of four: accent the first step; accent the last step.

Add these two bars together,

add claps and shouts to emphasise the accent.

How else can you emphasize the accent? With a gesture or a fall?

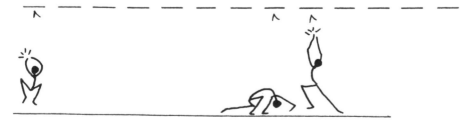

With a partner alternate the pattern. How many bar repeats make the easiest pattern?

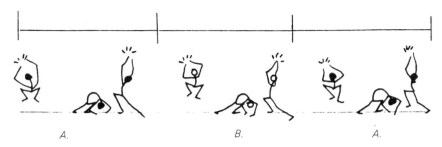

A.   B.   A.

Use this pattern alternatively to travel, to meet and part, to make a mock fight.

Repeat the pattern with no sound accompaniment. How do you keep in time?

Add the cymbal sound and movement to the drum beat. Which combination makes the most interesting dance? Which makes the easiest dance? Repeat the pattern several times to get the feel of it; try alternating sound and movement. Introduce the sound on the fourth repeat. Was your timing accurate?.

Example 4: Melodic sound

Use three chime bars. The different notes will make melodic pattern. Explore the shape of the melody using the shape of a movement. A rise in pitch is likely to match a rise in level, but not necessarily so.

Consider the possible curve of the sound.

Add other notes to extend the shape or elongate it.

What sounds suggest a circular or spiral pathway?

Add the drum beat to the chime bars to combine accent and shaping.

Draw the shape and the accent and use the drawing as a score for making music and dance. Add recorder sounds and chords on a piano or guitar; try using the strings in the piano.

159

Development

Create a sound sequence for the teacher's movement.

Two groups work together to create a sound and movement study.

Work in a similar way using voice and body percussion.

Listen to a piece of music, draw the shape of the sound and use the drawing as a dance score. Dance the score to the music.

Lesson 35: A Dance-Drama — The Story of Antigone (12+)

A dance — drama story in which the movement and sequence is directed by the music. Story: Anitigone. Music: Beethoven, 4th Piano Concerto, 2nd movement.

The music and the story are concerned with contrast, relationship and sequel. In the music, the orchestra and the piano declare their position and the piano triumphs in the dialogue that follows. The plot of the music resembles the relationship between Antigone and her guardian, Creon.

Antigone has two brothers who fight over whose turn it is to rule. Both die. The ruling brother, Eteocles, is declared a hero; and the contester, Polynices, is declared a traitor. According to the law, represented by Creon, no traitor is allowed funeral rites; the penalty is death. Antigone performs these rites for her brother and is condemned to death.

Creon's motif: The orchestra. This motif is mirrored by the statesmen and soldiers. Creon stands for law and order and military power. The gestures are disciplined and accurate and suggest the ceremonial handling of the sword and gestures of power. Steps, posture and gestures are economical, and stillness is equally powerful. The movements follow the orchestral chords. Use stage blocks to represent hierarchy.

The Creon group (half the class) works on a common motif which is manipulated for travel, entrances, forming groups and gestures.

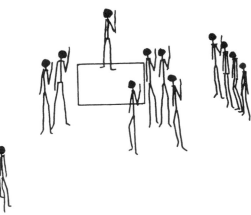

Antigone's motif: This is based on Greek funeral rites and symbolizes feelings associated with the sensing of things beyond the here and now. This includes the scattering of flowers to represent rebirth after death, the offering of the self upwards above the law of man, and submission to demonstrate humility. Each gesture completes its pathway but merges with the next to suggest continuity. Stillness expresses patient waiting rather than attention. The motif follows the piano motif. The Antigone group develops and manipulates the motif, bearing in mind the woman as chorus and the forming of the cave.

 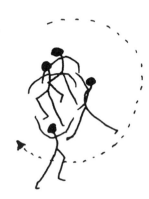

The sequence or dance script
The sequence is very tightly programmed according to the music. If the motifs are simple, logical and well practised there is scope for improvisation using cues in the music.
Preparation: Listen to the music and follow the script.

	Creon 1
Orchestra	The government assemble, Creon enters.

	Antigone 1
Piano	The women enter, stay in the peripheral space, and perform the rites.

	Creon 2
Orchestra	The guards appraise Creon of the rites, the people and the government show their anger and support for Creon.

	Antigone 2
Piano	Antigone is summoned and uses the motif to reaffirm her position which is mirrored by her women who nevertheless remain in the background unable to help.

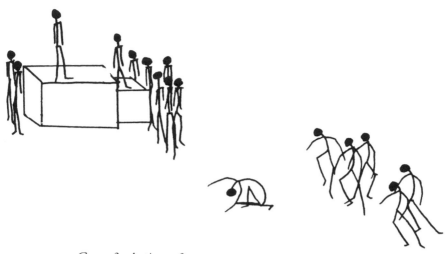

> *Creon 3, Antigone 3*
> Creon questions Antigone, she answers the accusations.

Orchestra
and
piano

> *Creon 4*
> Creon condemns Antigone.

> *Antigone 4*
> Antigone leaves, her woman are sympathetic but still unable to help, they form the cave which shuts in Antigone.

Creon and his supporters reassemble as if to confirm their belief in the justice of the act.

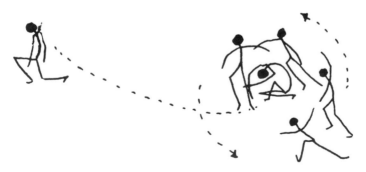

Development

The piano has a wandering passage as if finding its way. Haemon is Creon's son and betrothed to Antigone. Using this passage of music, he pleads for her life using a combination of the two motifs. The class or representative group develop this motif, all except Antigone and Creon become groups of people expressing attitudes towards Haemon (rather like the editorial column of a newspaper).

Haemon too is condemned and is shut in the cave to join Antigone in death.

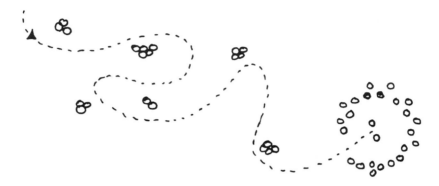

Development

The piano becomes agitated. Tiresias, a blind soothsayer, warns of the consequences of this judgment. In groups the class use movements to show their fear of the soothsayer's words, and illustrate his prophecies: disease; drought and failure of the food crops; death of the eldest son. Creon is unmoved but the people begin to doubt his wisdom.

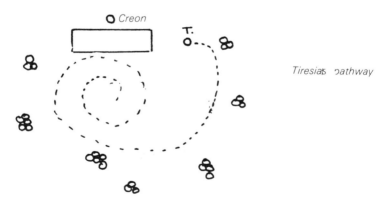

The orchestra becomes subdued. Creon takes a step down from his platform, a step that is the beginning of his fall and is recognized as such by the crowd. He makes his way slowly towards Anigone and Haemon, becoming weaker and weaker, as does the orchestra, and falls. Losing the leader, the crowd is unsure, and people group together for support, backing away from Creon. As the piano triumphs, so do Anigone and Haemon, confident in their rebirth.

Development and follow-up work

Find out more about the story of Anitgone and her family.

Consider other funeral rites, including our own.

Who are traitors and how are they punished?

Listen to the rest of the Beethoven concerto.

Include lighting, masks and speech in the performance.

People

Lesson 36: Work Actions (8+)

The quality of movement in work actions is determined by the function of the action, thus the shape/place/action/force/timing is given. A danced work action should embody these essential qualities but not be confused with a mimed work action in which the action seems real.

Begin by using ideas familiar to the children, perhaps miming such actions as sweeping or drinking tea. Extend their vocabulary by suggesting: pouring; polishing; stacking; carrying; threading; lifting.

Perform some of these actions using, if possible, objects and tools to explore the movement qualities of the real activity. Consider:

(i)   the placing of the body, particularly the hands;

(ii)   posture, the shape of the back;

(iii) the focus, the eyes and place of the head;

(iv) the shape of the action;

(v)   the emphasis — which part of the action is the most significant;

(iv) the timing — speed, stillness, and any pauses.

In twos, combine pulling and pushing in unison and opposition. Match the actions exactly, vary the levels and the placing, standing close or far apart. Develop this so each becomes a group or even half the class. Try cooperation leading to achievement, or opposition leading to winning. Explore other combinations such as lift and sink, throw and catch, put and take.

A: Perform one selected action as large/as small as possible whilst retaining the essential nature of the movement. Exaggerate qualities so that fast becomes very fast, and rounded becomes very rounded. Extract some of this material to develop a development motif; repeat it several times to learn the feel of the action. Perform the motif travelling / sitting / kneeling / turning / on a chair / in a small corner / on a stage block, to discover possible interpretations.

Figure 20   Pulling and pushing. Creating a movement motif based on work actions.

B: Observe people at work. Out of school ... on a building site, road works, railway station, wood yard, car dump. In school ... the caretaker, cleaner, dinner ladies — with their cooperation!

Develop the ability to really observe closely, by changing the viewpoint, drawing, making notes, discussion, taking photographs, recording, writing and reading fact sheets and descriptions.

Investigation and discussion: Why do people do different jobs? How do these jobs fit together? Is the work dangerous/easy/heavy/repetitive? How is it learnt?

Movement work: Use observation and notes to perform some of the activities. Repeat **A** and consider the effect of being informed.

Develop a motif to illustrate a work activity. Work with a partner to refine and polish this motif. Repeat the motif with variations such as change of size/place/speed. Work with a partner, in threes, or in a small group to combine related actions. Learn and perform each other's, or interrelate the individual motifs. Choreograph these motifs to create a dance study, paying attention to the start and finish, for example:

Beginning — consider starting one at a time, small, with pauses.
Middle section — large movements, unison, intensity.
Conclusion — reverse the beginning, suddenly freeze, slow down, come together with a common motif.

Work actions with objects

Find any available object such as a shoe, jumper, bag, or book. Collect, hold, carry, and place the object as if it were very fragile. Note the shape of the body, the speed, the pathway and the focus; also note the class atmosphere. Share one such object in a small or large group using speech to encourage careful handling. Explore ways in which several people work together to do this, such as taking turns, following and supporting a leader, or taking different roles.

Whilst having due regard for the actual object, handle it as if it were heavy / dangerous / hot / alive / precious / explosive / a secret / disgusting / smelly — and be aware of the change in language, mood and relationship. (With an inexperienced class, foam balls are helpful alternatives).

A directed activity

Imagine stacking shelves in a supermarket. The teacher gives verbal and rhythmic accompaniment, describing the work and establishing the insistent continuity, for example:

> 'pick up the tin,
> stand it on the shelf,
> reach for another,
> and pass on the tray'

as in

> 'gonna jump down, turn around, pick a bale of cotton'.

Children make a percussive rhythm to accompany the action, others make a chant. Develop the sequence by adding more related jobs, e.g. A × 4; (A + B) × 4, (A + B + C) × 4, (A + B + C + D) × 4.

Work actions developing from cross-curricular study

Example 1: Crawling to the coal face in a nineteenth-century mine. (Some workers crawled half a mile on hands and knees, and pay began when they reached the coal face.) Try crawling under desks and tables without moving them in any way. Crawl through gaps and tunnels using staging or other bodies. Crawl as if in a hurry to escape a gas leak, as if sick or injured, as if dedicated to the work.

Example 2: Pulling a rope together, as if hauling in fishing lines or sails. Pull using different body parts and positions; vary the level and the relationship with others. Pull as if the work is joyous, as if celebrating success, or as if desperate as in a storm.

Development

Develop the study by adding other events or changing the situation. Use music such as Negro spirituals or sea shanties to accompany the action. Define the space by using markings on the gym floor, or marking space with blocks, chairs, or people. Work on transitions between work as drudgery and the same work as lighthearted. Bring the work to a climactic finish by increasing the speed/numbers/size/force.

Use the study in a context, such as refugees; pioneers; prisoners; disaster at sea; harvest; rebuilding.

Compare people with machines. See Lesson 52.

Lesson 37: Man and the Environment: Journeys (Any Age)

This could relate to inter-curricular studies about current world affairs, exploration and discovery, fiction, or history.

Movement vocabulary and improvisation practice
Travel across the surface of the floor as if it were sticky; slimy; hot; icy; covered in thorns; the home of a poisonous reptile.

Travel as if wearing different footwear such as heavy boots; tight-fitting shoes; bare sore feet; sloppy slippers; snow shoes.

Explore movement actions to overcome imagined obstacles, such as slithering through drainpipes; breaking through barbed wire; climbing walls (use the shape and action of the body, not the effect of height); pushing through dense undergrowth or through heavy doors; crossing an open plain.

If necessary, use gym apparatus to study kinds of actions.

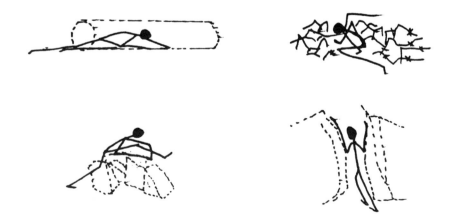

Overcome these obstacles as if in an imaginary situation: escaping; hiding; looking for clues; in a minefield; in a freezing wind.

If the room can be blacked out, use torches to assemble groups and to establish a focus or atmosphere.

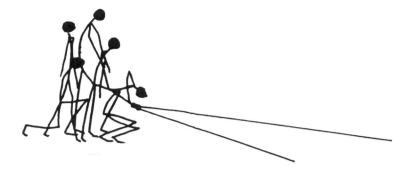

Explore ways in which a group can share a journey: lead; follow; guide; take turns; relay; move in a block or single file.

Stepping stones

Each imagine stepping stones across the space. Organize the work so that all move at the same time — children will accept crossing paths.

Give each stone a different quality: almost too small; wobbly; slippery; huge; occasionally submerged; a large distance from others; several close together.

Improvise and recap.

In twos, one has crossed and instructs the other as if he is deaf; afraid; stupid; or does not know the language.

In fours, all cross using the *exact* pathway. Imagine strong, weak or injured members. Add baggage; a following enemy; darkness; secrecy; an accident; the discovery that this is the wrong river. Incorporate a real prop: a rope; an umbrella; a suitcase.

Development: link with humanities

Research an environment or an example of man's experience found in literature, history or current events.

Develop individual and group travel actions according to the context.

168

Lesson 38: Man and the Environment: Deserts (8-13)

Deserts represent about a third of the world's surface. Weathering makes very small sand particles that can be carried by the wind, polishing each other to make smooth surfaces and sharp edges. Wind-blown sand flows to form ripples, and eddies to expose huge flat mounds of bare earth that cover vegetation and even habitation.

Part 1: The movement of desert sand

Dancers lie as if they are the desert floor; there is no wind or sign of life, only utter stillness with an occasional small change in the shape of the surface. If possible use sheets and lengths of soft material to cover the bodies and lighting to emphasize shadows; create a still silence.

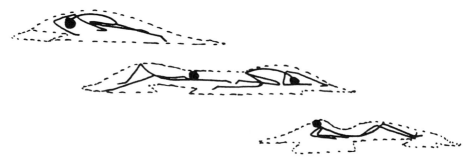

Stand aside to observe and develop the movement of the cloth or bodies.

Use these same shapes to suggest the flow of the sand across the space as it advances or retreats. Find movements to show eddying; denuding; accumulating; an ever-changing sand-sea.

Investigate the effect of neglect or careful planting in desert areas.

Part 2: Drought

Make shapes to suggest trees that severely lack water: stark branches, peeling bark, uncovered roots, broken limbs, fallen trunks.

Gradually increase the number of shapes to suggest a long period of drought.

Use percussion instruments and improvised instruments to make a sound sequence to suggest a vast dry place. Screw paper; snap sticks; drop beans into a tin.

Add sound-making to the movement scene, maintaining the look and feel of the environment so that instrumentalists lie or huddle together.

Part 3

Isolated figures emerge, cross the space and disappear as if on a fruitless or very long journey. Consider the posture and pathway of each traveller. Where is the entrance and exit?

Part 4

Imagine a mirage. What might such a traveller long to see? Select ideas that can be created in movement: a city; a market place; a crowd; luscious vegetation.

the skyline of a city

Develop the mirage so that it forms and dissolves and the sand surface is reestablished.

Make slides for a projector or OHP to project an image onto the floor, the wall, the dancers.

Improvise with old blankets or buy a silk parachute.

Write and use spoken descriptions of the landscape and of human feelings.

Story

Understanding Story Content and Developing Movement Expression

Choose a story that contains passages crucial to the plot or idea that can be interpreted in movement. The dance work must reveal the essence of the story and not distort its content, otherwise children may always remember the wrong interpretation. The movement exploration of a story is memorable, requiring concern for accuracy and worthwhileness. Folk tales, myths and legends, parables and ballads provide good source material.

Lesson 39: Myth: Demeter and Persephone; The Seasons (Any Age)

Ref: Collins Myth and Legend Book, Farmer and McCallum.

Part 1: Wherever Demeter and Persephone wander, flowers bloom and there is sunshine and happiness.

Avoid representing the wanderers. Sunshine and joy are more difficult to explore in dance than darkness and despair and need structure. Either create a folk dance that is celebratory or explore the unfolding of plant life.

For example: observe tight buds, closely folded and dormant. Notice that buds are evident on some plants in the summer before so that winter is a resting time rather than a dead time. Collect, observe and draw buds.

Movement: Explore individual and group shapes, tightly closed.

Observe and investigate the unfolding of leaf and flower buds. Look at a film speeded up, 'undo' plant specimens. Use this investigation to create unfolding body/group shapes. Consider which part moves. How far open can the shape become? Does it begin at the centre or at the end? Is the unfolding uniform or uneven? Consider extension in size and shape using stepping or stage blocks to increase length and height, which might also involve balance.

Choreograph the class shape to open successively as if Demeter and Persephone had passed through the space. Do they pause; stay together; repeat a pathway? Could an audience imagine their journey?

171

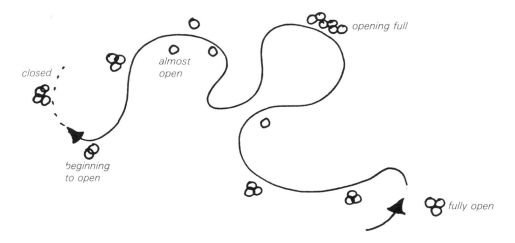

Part 2: The earth gapes open as Hades kidnaps Persephone.

Avoid any mime of kidnapping, since this has little to do with the story. Concentrate on the change from the earth's flowering surface to a void.

Create a stepping pattern to form a group and then a class circle which increases in size to embrace all the space, and decreases and disperses, becoming still, as if leaving no trace of Persephone's disappearance.

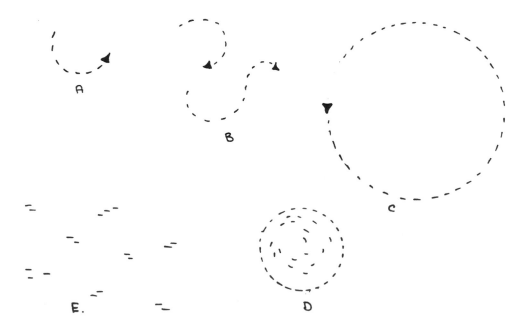

Part 3: Demeter is distressed and the earth withers.

The world is cold and dark, and land is empty and people are sick and unhappy.

Movement: Observe the shape of winter trees, of frost and dead things; imagine the shape of stillness and silence.

Move as if withering/twisting in agony/curling/fragmenting/falling. Explore hand movements that beg for sustanance, seek help, are rejected and gradually succumb. Repeat these movements using the whole body.

Explore opposite actions and the transition between them. Consider the change in attitude and reverse the order so that, for example, hope becomes despair, and fatigue becomes recovery.

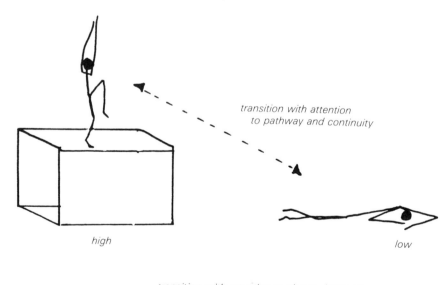

*transition with attention
to pathway and continuity*

high

low

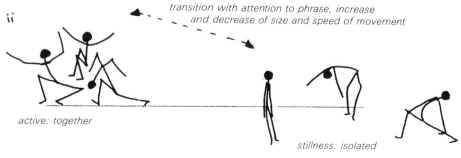

*transition with attention to phrase, increase
and decrease of size and speed of movement*

ii

active: together

stillness: isolated

Part 4

Persephone returns for seven months ... Part 1; goes back to Hades for five months ... Part 2; returns to earth ... Part 1.

Combine the studies to complete the story performance.

Follow-up work

Write and narrate story links.

Create music for summer and winter using contrasting sounds and instruments.

Listen to examples in recorded music.

Visual art: contrast colour, texture and shape.

Investigate associated rites, such as planting and harvesting customs; the making and burying of corn dollies; the association of poppies with cornfields and their colour with death and resurrection.

Lesson 40: Parable: The Good Samaritan (7–13)

The following example illustrates the importance of selecting essential content and appropriate movement.

Part 1: 'A certain man went from Jerusalem to Jericho and fell among thieves.

Consider journeying through dangerous country, in remote terrain offering little comfort but providing cover for thieves. An example is a rocky barren place. Look at some rock or stone samples. Explore the weight, structure and texture.

Make body shapes that capture the timelessness of stone and make shapes that threaten and induce a feeling of unease and fear. Experiment with individual and group shapes; select, refine, and position them.

Move a person (teacher or child) between these rock-like shapes as if on a journey. When not observed the rocks slightly alter position so that the traveller feels afraid as if the stones might be alive.

Change the stone slowly to robbers and move stealthily along the pathway of the journey to create a route for the traveller. The movements are reminiscent of the rocks so that movement seems unobserved.

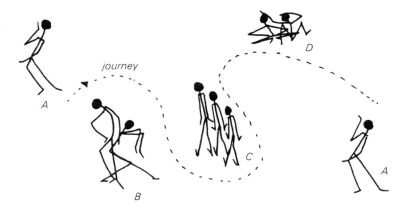

Repeat this sequence with an imagined traveller whose journey is made clear by the movement of the thieves/rocks.

Explore hand gestures to suggest robbery and violence. Make a series of still gestures and add word accompaniment, for example 'come here', 'give me that', 'hold him', 'grab his coat'. Use these words to create a still image of thieves who have been photographed as they group around the imagined traveller. Avoid body contact or any suggestion of real violence by concentrating on the hands.

The traveller is then suggested by a cloth or garment and the thieves take up the original rock shapes leaving the space all but empty and deserted. Work on the transition from thief group to rocks to sustain the sense of unease and stillness.

Part 2: 'And when the priest saw him, he passed by on the other side'.
Work on focus and relationship. If necessary use several groups, each with a garment.

Place the garment in the centre of the floor. Find ways of walking past it without recognizing its existence: as if in a hurry or busy; focus elsewhere; preoccupation with personal situation; blind.

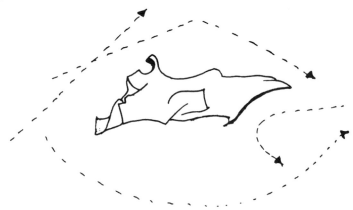

Select and repeat some of these ideas adding a slight interest in the cloth but still without involvement. Develop that interest, show and discuss.

Repeat but freeze as soon as one dancer makes a gesture of commitment. (Direct or improvise.) Consider the group formation and develop movements to express the relationship to the committed, such as unaware, supportive, or taking an opposite view. What might each be thinking? Write these phrases and use as voice accompaniment for the group shape.

Discuss the long-term commitment that might follow the initial gesture, such as the Samaritan leaving money at the inn for follow-up care. Discuss contemporary examples, including famine relief and owning pets.

Part 3: 'A certain Samaritan saw him and had compassion on him, ... he bound his wounds, ... brought him to the inn, and on the morrow gave twopence to the host saying "take care of him".'
Lie on the floor as if damaged or ill. Consider kinds of injury and effects of illness.

Learn first-aid treatment and the recovery position. Take turns to be the patient. Repeat selected actions in slow motion and with the utmost care and cooperation.

Take the part of injured or helper, the latter adding the approach and initial recognition; hold the finish position.

These three parts may be joined to make a dance performance of the story although the experience itself is more important. Groups and individuals may select sequences and roles, for example, a group might retain rock shapes for the thieves to move around.

Follow-up work: Discuss the implications of involvement with others; learn first-aid procedures and visit an ambulance station.

Consider the difference between helping people we know and making ANY contact with strangers. Learn how to get help. Discuss ways of being supportive at home and in school.

Lesson 41: Legend: The First Sunrise (Ideas 5+; Whole Dance 7–9)

This legend is from *The Dance and The Drum* by Elizabeth and John Paynter, published by Universal Edition.

This story is a very good example of a context that lends itself to dance interpretation. There are, of course, many ways of using the story; the following is an example of selected passages in which the essence of the story is used to define and structure the movement whilst providing opportunity for improvisation and personal expression.

Part 1

When the world was made the sky was so close to the earth that no light could get in. Everyone had to crawl around in the darkness collecting things to eat with their bare hands. Living was difficult and uncomfortable. There was no space where the birds could fly.

Introductory movement

Explore movements that maintain close contact with the floor; roll, crawl, bend, creep. Use the fingers to reach and take. Make the fingers and arms look twice as long. Combine gestures and travel pathways and freeze at the point of longest reach; recover using closing-in movements. If necessary, scatter pieces of paper to be collected.

Move as if the ceiling is only three feet high: use imagination or ropes or sheets to show the level of the ceiling.

Figure 21   The First Sunrise. 'Everyone had to crawl around in the darkness collecting things to eat with their bare hands'.

177

Compose and combine individual motifs for

(a) moving across the floor,
(b) reach and reach, over-reaching and falling;
(c) crawling together for comfort.

Part 2

Then the magpies, who were the cleverest of the birds, had an idea. Working together they could, perhaps, raise the sky a little and so make room.

They collected long sticks. Then slowly and all together, using the sticks, they began to push the sky upwards away from the earth. Resting, first on low boulders and then on higher ones, they lifted the sky until there was room for everyone to stand upright.

Figure 22   'The magpies lifted the sky until there was room for everyone to stand upright'.

Introductory movement: The Magpies: Watch, recall watching and discuss the way magpies and crows move. Use this observation as reference for bodily movement (but NOT pretending to be magpies).

Define different movement qualities, for example:

Strutting: Consider the posture; lifting and placing the feet; pathway and phrase. Where should the focus be?

Swooping: Consider travel or gesture with a downward path; where the starting and finishing positions are; what the shape of the body is. How quick should this be and how can you share the space with others?

Balancing and lifting: Consider body shape; getting into and out of balance; where your support is. Use the hands as if holding a stick. How many directions upward can you use? Can you reach without always using straight arms?

Create an individual sequence that uses some of these bird-like motifs. Incorporate the idea of gathering sticks — how big? from where to where? — and finally lifting them.

Perform the sequence so that you finish in groups of three and hold a finished position.

Part 3

With all their strength they tried to get the sky even higher. Struggling to do so they split the sky open, and through the broken cloud came a first few rays of light. The gap widened, revealing the sun. The magpies burst into glorious song as the broken pieces of sky floated away in clouds. Daybreak and the first dawn chorus began.

Introductory movement: Look at the movement of steam, or smoke from a snuffed candle. Move as if weightless (see Lesson 16). Move hands as if they are trailing mist; be sustained and smooth. Add gentleness to walking. The posture is elevated and the focus across the space.

In a trio, follow a leader to create a trailing mist-like group with space between you. As you travel look forwards and backwards to watch where you are going and where you come from. Turn the head slowly and evenly. Move very slowly.

Slowly combine all the trios to spiral into a single 'cloud' group. Remain still, then suddenly step back to reveal a small hole in the centre. Keeping the trios, gradually step away from the hole so that it gets bigger and fills the room. Look upward as if the space above is unlimited; finish with still groups at the edge of the space.

Performance

Use movement to explore the story. Although there is no performance each lesson/section reaches a level of completion. If the story takes three lessons, discuss the previous passage, but do not spend time recalling the movement itself.

Three classes may each contribute a passage, thereby taking on the role of crawling creatures, the magpies, and the sky.

Narrate the story as it is performed.

It is tempting to add masks and finger gloves, but the movement is more important and likely to be sufficient.

Fantasy

Introduction

Dance ideas about fantasy and magic provide opportunities for imaginative freedom and creative invention but must be based on knowledge and skill if sentimentality and imitative mediocrity is to be avoided. The lessons in this book show that investigation of content and movement is an essential basis for dance work and this is no less true of dance about magic, dreams, fairyland or science fiction. The successful creation of a fictitious monster, whether in cardboard or movement, must be based on knowledge of the structure and behaviour of real animals.

The kind of imagining in a lesson must also be considered and planned. Imagination that persuades the children to believe something falsely or inaccurately has no place in the classroom, and neither has imagination that takes the children out of themselves so that they are frightened by the masked witch or the monster 'outside the window'.

Healthy imagination is based on knowing or coming to know. Examples are imagining what it is like to be in someone else's shoes, or visualizing the possible however impossible it may seem. It is also about being able to develop the imagined ideas in a communicative form and to harness the outcome (see also the section on creating in Chapter One).

Magic

Magical practices are functional and are intended to arouse emotions and beliefs to serve practical purposes, for example, a rain dance to make the crop grow, or a war dance to believe in the right to fight and to feel invincible.

In this sense magic is useful, as was dance in the past when it nearly always served magic purposes. 'Magic' dance is still evident in processions and ritual movement connected with law, sport, government, and religion.

Dance is magical when it makes something special, for example:

- A place — by extending the approach route as in a labyrinth; by defining a boundary as in the theatre or church; by particular behaviour.
- A person — by adding gestures, costume, attendants and objects.

- An event — by adding procession, music, clothes, particular actions; by nominating a time and place.

Events in life are made special through prolonged preparation and anything that extends this preparation is magical. The 'magic' of Christmas is created by the extra preparation of food and the decoration of rooms — including classrooms! The magic of a present is increased by the wrapping and the form of presentation.

Lesson 42: The Magic of Christmas: The Story of the Three Wise Men (7–13)

This lesson deals with the Special Person and the journey and the visit of the Three Wise Men or Three Kings. The object of their journey — the infant Jesus — is afforded specialness.

Read 'The Journey of the Magi' by T.S. Eliot. Magi is also a term for a Persian priest versed in astrology and magic.

Part 1: The movement insignia of each king
Imagine the home of each king. What movements might one do in a land that is

(i)   hot desert: perhaps covering oneself from the heat of the sun, and looking across long distances;

(ii)   steep and stony mountains: climbing and treading carefully with help from others;

(iii)   dangerous country inhabited by thieves and bandits: carrying a sword and guarding belongings.

In groups create movement motifs that identify each king, and use the motif for travelling, studying the sky, and paying homage. Add to each king a group of attendants who use their king's motif. The kings and their retinue might well be the whole class.

Part 2: The Journey
Create a pathway for each king which may be identical or very different.

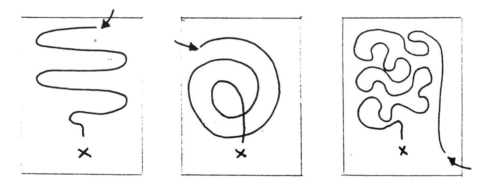

The pathway extends the time and the distance and gives an opportunity for performance. Consider the entrance, the pathway, and the destination. The travel actions may develop from the motif and include a dramatic happening such as a robbery or a sandstorm.

Do the kings meet up or stay separate? Is there an order of seniority? Does any part of the journey need music, onlookers, porters, or documents?

Part 3: The special place: the manger in the inn
Where is the best position in the hall, the most important or the humblest? How big is the place and how close are people allowed to get? What shape is it? Is it guarded by shepherds, angels, inn people? If so how do they arrive and leave? The place could be entirely imaginary created by what goes on around it.

Part 4: The special visit and the gifts

How is the gift carried and placed? Is it guarded and does it have a special carrier with attendants?

How and where do people move and stand?

How do the kings and their attendants leave? Do they repeat the same journey in reverse, or is it different after seeing the Christ child?

What happens to the special place? Do the people there remain still or leave? How?

Look at Nativity scene pictures by, for example, El Greco or Raphael, and consider the grouping of the characters.

Investigate behaviour in special places such as taking off or putting on hats, removing shoes, wearing special clothes, washing hands, saying special words of address.

Map a possible journey and write a guide. Cost it.

Set the performance to sung carols.

Add a costume motif to accompany each movement motif, such as a map, a sword, and a stave.

Dream images

In dreams and personal fantasies, imagined experience evokes real emotions such as anxiety, fears and wishes which appear as images taken from parts of experience. Unlike real experience these images are not subject to rational thought, so that fragments from different times and places can fuse and substances can assume impossible qualities, the incompatible coming together.

Art images, of which dance is an example, are also of ideas felt, but unlike dream images, the feelings are consciously conceived, given form and presented.

Exploring dream images is a way of understanding the relation between feelings and the image of feeling, between feeling and form. Dance has a special link with dreams because its use of space and time can create illusions within space and time. Thus shapes can form, change, and dissolve, and sequences can appear to reverse their order in time, bodies can join and separate, and gravity seem to be overcome.

Movement and dream qualities: introductory work

Make a starting position that is negative and 'says' as little as possible. Move into a positive shape and back again, add changes of shape and gradually include other people, combine ideas so that the sequence seems to come and go.

Move isolated parts of the body as if only that part was alive, move from one body part to another, repeat using individual bodies as separated parts of a whole group.

Travel backwards using a forward walk — this feels and looks as if the past and future are merged.

Consider anxiety dreams in which that which is sought is always just beyond reach, like running for a moving bus or walking without advancing. Try a slow motion fall which goes on and on before reaching the floor. Try getting up with body parts getting higher but never the whole body. Advance to meet a partner and pass without recognition.

Discuss dream images and select those that can be danced, each group create a dream sequence, join the sequences so that they gradually emerge and dancers change from one thing to another or leave in the middle of a movement. Sustain movements or images to give a timeless quality.
Examples of dream images:

- (i) being chased
- (ii) falling
- (iii) getting nowhere
- (iv) drowning
- (v) being ignored by others
- (vi) being trapped

Do not attempt to portray the dreamer or people snoring or tossing bedclothes; focus on the illusion of the dream-like state.

185

Lesson 43: A Dream Collage: A Midsummer Night's Dream *(9+)*

This is a dance study to explore and illustrate Titania's dream in *A Midsummer Night's Dream*.

> And with this juice I'll streak her eyes,
> And make her full of hateful fantasies.

Discuss the context.
Discuss understanding of 'hateful fantasies'.
Consider movement ideas and images, for example

- hands that grasp and steal possessions,
- hands that blindfold,
- bodies that are grotesque and distorted,
- eyes that stare and watch wherever you are,
- fingers that poke, point, accuse or mock,
- faces that grimace,
- voices that tempt and scorn, that laugh in ridicule.

Explore the shape of the hands and fingers, move and freeze with sudden changes in direction and level. Move so that joints appear ugly and uncomfortable as if the body was deformed, with turned-up feet, hunched shoulders, and twisted torso. Let parts hang as if broken.

In twos and threes find combinations that emphasize grotesque shapes by contrast, opposition, and extension.

Discuss words that are linked with ugliness and unpleasant things. Write words and phrases and speak them in appropriate voices.

Make faces that are haggard, scowling, gaunt, warped, squeezed.

Use the hands as if holding objects that are slimy, alive, poisonous, tentacled, smelly.

Create a class movement collage that is a moving image of Titania's dream.

Choreograph a group of movements as if on a flat screen; make the whole movement study a series of flat images.

arms and hands move like a swarm of bees

eyes that stare and follow in unison

shapes that collapse and twist back up

Reality

Creating an art form makes us conceive things in abstraction whether it be in metaphor, imitation, or transformation. That the abstraction has significance and is comprehensible is due to its reference to reality. A dance about captivity, whether psychological or actual, must be based on a knowledge and understanding of captivity, a dance about machines or man and mechanization must be based on the structure and function of machines. This point is made through all the lessons in this chapter and illustrates the contribution of art-making to understanding and insight.

Lesson 44: Machines: A Bicycle (Any Age)

It is essential that the children have first-hand experience of a machine such as a bicycle, which is easily come by in a school. Several children could share their bicycles with the class. The bicycle includes examples of levers, cogs, gears, wheels, pumps and chains. Find out about machines. Stand a bicycle upside down and look at it, discuss, draw, label, and investigate the mechanical parts.

Introductory movement
Explore pushing and pulling movements. Change size, place, direction, and body part.

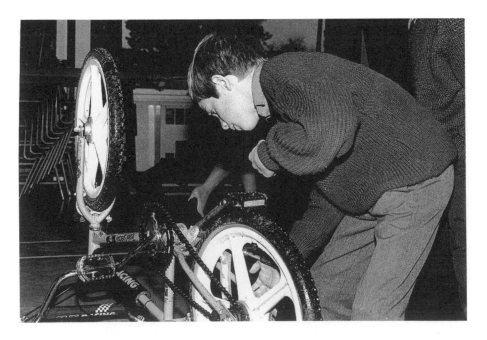

Figure 23   A machine dance starting with the investigation of a bicycle.

Work with a partner to explore action and reaction, pushing and being pushed, pulling and being pulled.

Work in threes to explore passive and active weight, and alternating sequence.

Find body parts that can rotate. Can you change direction without stopping?

Examine the movement of your joints and limbs; locate levers, hinges, balls and sockets. Find actions that are machine-like: push, pull, heave, rock, roll, tap, stamp, punch, carry, tilt. Repeat some of these movements to find the rhythm.

Return to the bicycle

Examine the function of the brake lever. What is the connection between the cable, the brake blocks, and the turning wheel? How is the cable constructed and why?

Using a group, magnify the action in slow motion using body movement, each taking a different part of the brake system. Is the action simultaneous? Can it work in reverse?

Examine the gearwheel. How many teeth has each wheel? How do they move together and what is the effect?

Use three bodies and find ways of interacting to demonstrate the differences in rotation and speed. Use slow motion and magnify the size.

189

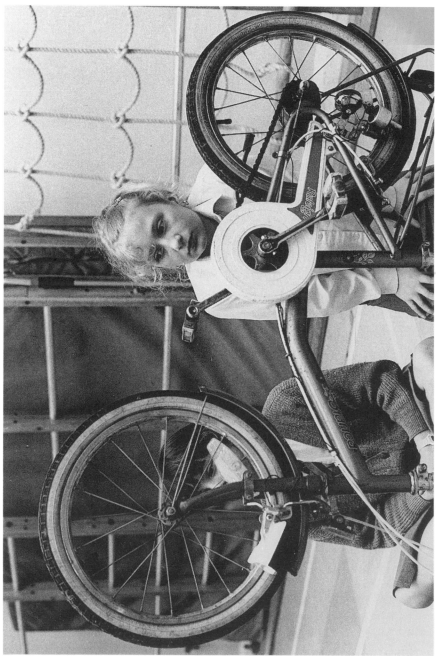

Figure 24   The bicycle includes examples of levers, cogs, wheels, and chains.

Figure 25   Exploring passive and active weight.

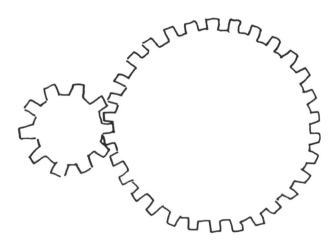

Examine the chain system. Notice how the pedals cause the chain wheel to turn, how the chain is put into tension, and how the motion is transmitted to the rear wheel.

191

Figure 26   Interpreting the function of the bicycle brake lever.

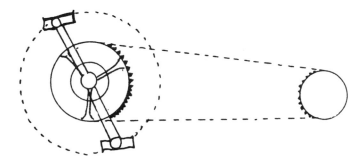

Use a group of dancers to simulate the action of the pedals. Magnify the size and adjust the action to bodily movements. Pay particular attention to the interaction.

Follow-up work

Investigate the ratio between the pedal action and the wheel turning. Calculate the ratio between the pedal action and distance covered.

Look at the mechanics of a hand sewing-machine. What is the connection between the drive, the up and down movement of the needle, and the shuttle? What makes the stitch?

Development: a class machine

Using introductory investigation of machinery and movement ideas, create a class machine. Start with one central body and add others section by section so that the parts interact. The machine may represent an actual machine or combine ideas.

How does the machine start and stop? How can you be repetitive without giddiness or monotony? Do parts have different actions that alternate? Do they interrelate successively or simultaneously? Does power and speed remain constant?

Investigate machine sounds; using voice, percussion, and recorded machines, make a sound accompaniment for the class study.

Develop the study to include a happening: a power failure, a broken link, metal fatigue, friction and overheating.

What is the difference between people working and machines working? Choreograph a dance study about labour and mechanization.

Possible context work could include the Industrial Revolution, slavery, serfs, the development of tools and weapons, folk dance, and work actions.

Lesson 45: Magnetic Force (7+)

Magnetic poles always occur in pairs, the north and the south seeking pole. Unlike poles attract and like poles repel. The region near a pole is the magnetic field which can be seen as a pattern using a sheet of paper and iron filings.

Heated wax paper can be used to fix the pattern. The greater the distance, the less attractive the force. A magnet will only attract certain metals.

Although evidence of force can be seen, the force itself is invisible. In this sense it is like the force of attraction between two people or between a person and a desired object. Let the children handle two magnets to feel the power of the force as they try to bring like poles together or unlike poles apart.

Imitate this force with the two hands, repeat using a partner's hand.

Find out about the earth's magnetism, and electromagnets. Use a compass to map-read or follow directions.

Introductory movement
(See also Lessons 1, 2, and 3 on body awareness.)

Repeat the work with the hand moving like a magnet; repeat the movement using the whole body. Working with a partner, maintain the same distance as you travel, turn, or change level and body weight support.

Move towards an object as if being pulled against your will. Use different body parts as the point of 'capture' keeping the body as far in the opposite direction as possible.

Join a partner to extend the length of pull.

Try to enter a 'magnetic field' which repels your body.

Observe the speed with which iron filings respond to the magnet, and study the shape of clustered filings. What happens when the force is removed?

Create group formations that suddenly become energized and then collapse.

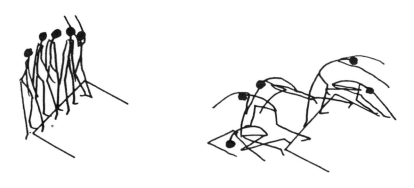

In small groups, select three movement/magnet ideas to create a study. Consider the order of sequence and transitions.

Show the study to the class. What other titles could be given to the study? They might include greed, hunger, magical powers, spells, love, hatred. Does a title add to the meaning? Can the dance be modified according to the title without changing the original task? What would happen if other groups were added and in what capacity?

How can the invisible force be intensified? With music, lighting, spoken words, more silence, more sustained movement, more opposition?

Lesson 46: Food — Yeast and Bread-Making (Any Age)

Food as a topic of study should include investigation about the provision and preparation of food, its production and distribution. This is about the economics and science of food and is not appropriate for dance. The structure of food such as bread, fruit, and vegetables, however, is a good starting point for dance since it is about form, and how that form is sensed.

The dance lesson provides opportunities to examine, interpret, and understand, for example, protective shells, protected seeds, growth and decay.

Although yeast was used to ferment alcohol and to leaven bread, its nature was a mystery for thousands of years. An early English name for yeast or balm was 'godisgood', implying a blessing.

Children explore the notion of growth, and of expansion created by making holes. They make dough, using its plasticity to shape it. Notice flexibility, joining, separating, twisting, and stretching. The plasticity of the dough gives a better feel of movement than plasticine or clay.

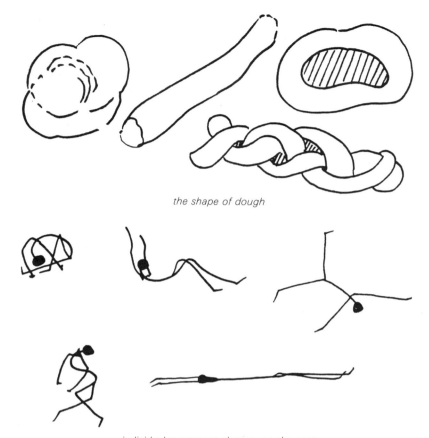

the shape of dough

individual movement shapes, on the spot

group movements in place, smooth changing shape

Shapes can be recalled to create floor patterns: stepping, rolling, running, turning. Floor patterns danced by a group to entwine, plait, interweave, encircle and double back; retaining the smooth transitions of the dough. Shapes can be squeezed, pressed and pulled, imaginarily or actually, as in kneading.

When the bread is baked, the yeast is killed and the shape of the bread is fixed. Make shapes that stay still, and shapes that are sliced, yet retain the sense of stillness.

Lesson 47: Water (Any Age)

Ancient philosophy regarded water as one of the four elements, the others being earth, fire and air. How many elements do we know of now?

Investigate the physical properties of water. It is an example of liquid and has a degree of freedom limited by the close proximity of the molecules. It will accept the shape of any vessel that contains it.

Observe the way colour dissolves in water using ink and dye and an overhead projector. Try to capture this fluidity in bodily movement. As a group establish some relationship with each other but move loosely around and 'flow' across the space together. Flow over and around obstacles such as stage blocks. Change level and position; lead with particular body parts.

Gas molecules move independently in complete disorder, collision with walls and each other producing atmospheric pressure.

Try collision movements in slow motion and with no actual body contact. Occupy the whole available space as a class/group/person.

Ice is the solid state of water. Molecules are closely joined so that shapes become dense and fixed. Explore group shapes with some contact and with no body contact. Move from one shape to another retaining group structure and sense of stability. Consider glaciers flowing and breaking into ice flows.

Make a sequence by joining these ideas together to suggest ice forming, melting into liquid and becoming water vapour.

Discuss the contribution of evaporation and condensation to the support of life.

Use this sequence to illustrate topic work about the water cycle, linking written work, collage, and drama.

Rain
Watch rain falling. Why does it appear as lines? Raindrops vary in size from 0.02 mm to 0.5 mm. Find words to describe different kinds of rain: drizzle, spotting, dripping, drenching, pouring, raining cats and dogs, teeming down, torrential.

Watch drops of water as they land on water.

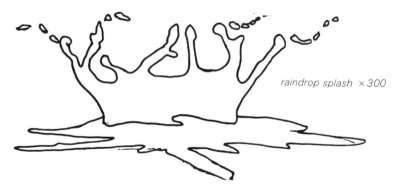

raindrop splash ×300

Watch puddles forming and water collecting on window panes and in gutters.

Make rain music. Tap fingers on the floor increasing speed and amount of hand used. Use hand movements to suggest a little/a lot of rain falling (this is more appropriate than running) ... add arms, and whole bodies, if necessary in slow motion. Add rain noise and rain words to create a raining atmosphere. Use this to make a rain dance. Magic dance often imitates the phenomena it wishes to influence.

Observe ripples in a bowl of water; in a puddle; in a large pond. Find out what ripples are and where they go. Explore movements that ripple through the fingers, the body, the group, and the class. Try group ripples in a confined space and in a large space using the whole playground or a corridor. Explore the use of touch, sight, and sound to communicate within the group.

Lesson 48: Reflections (9–13)

In this example the movement content is explored before the context. The work includes two ideas, spatial dimensions (see glossary) and reflected images.

Exploring up and down

Establish a relationship with the floor. This is a safe place, you cannot fall, it is concrete and permanent. Choose your own bit of floor, make it yours with close body contact, leave it unwilling and return with relief.

Focus on the space above and imagine the space beyond the roof, even beyond the sky ... this is infinite space and is unknown ... how do you move towards it from your position on the floor? Make a rising and sinking sequence using this notion of the safe floor and the unknown space above.

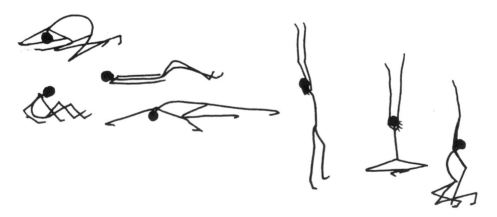

Exploring left and right, outward and inward

Move the right side of the body towards the left side. This encloses the body centre and focuses on the self, on privacy. Watch how people move when they are afraid or unhappy. Move the right side towards the right: this embraces the outside world, including others in it. Join these two movements using open extension and closed contraction which might also make you turn outwards or inwards.

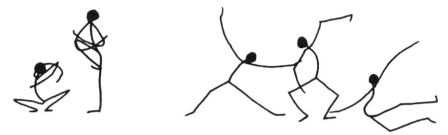

Exploring forward and backward

Work with a partner to involve the feeling of meeting and parting. Advance slowly or quickly, with anticipation, and consider the place of body front and focus. Retreat slowly or quickly, consider the distance and moment when contact is broken. Both may move or only one partner; you may even cross paths, and sustain some bodily contact.

Development

These three dimensions produce six locations which can be abbreviated in notation to H/D/R/L/F/B. Select three locations and combine them to create a motif, paying attention to transitional pathways and related attitudes.

For example:

H.R.L.

Use these individual motifs to create a dance study based on the idea of reflections. Well-prepared movement vocabulary will readily and quickly enable the children to achieve a satisfying interpretation, choreography and performance.

Suggested interpretations

Exactly mirror a partner's motif; join the two to make a longer sequence. Explore placing and relationship.

The whole class mirror one such sequence, face a common or varying front. Space evenly or use different levels by introducing staging etc.

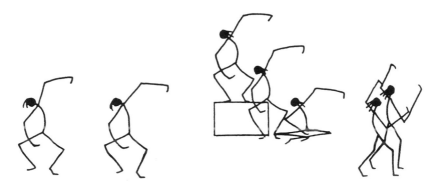

Combine group studies to mix mirrored images with single images. Perform sequences in canon as if the reflection is passing or is being formed.

Each dancer perform a part of an image which eventually becomes wholly complete.

Select a common motif, each select a part which is then distorted to create another movement phrase. Distortion is achieved by changing the speed/size/level/body part, and by adding repetition. Distorted images can be further exaggerated by adding costume such as masks and gloves, or lighting to create shadows and silhouettes.

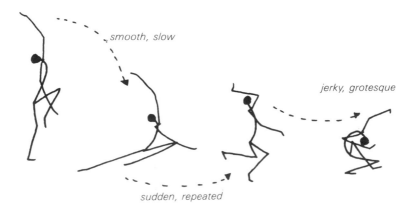

smooth, slow

jerky, grotesque

sudden, repeated

The sequence, although effective, is simple enough to adjust to music, using music cues for the different sequences. Suggested music: Debussy, *Reflets dans l'eau*; Britten, 'Dawn' from *Peter Grimes*.

Lighting: project watery light on the dancers or a back screen using a clear tray to hold water and an overhead projector.

Related study could include science, light and reflected images; fine art appreciation (Monet, Turner); self-images in mirrors and shop windows, and distorted ones in spoons; printing, negative and positive images, blots;

Observation, drawing and writing in the natural environment — look at the effect of ripples and wind.

Lesson 49: Water, Sea, and Storm (7–13+)

Observation of the real sea is important. Children must sense the sea through touch, sight and sound. They must feel the wind on the face and the feel of the motion of the water. If the sea is not available, the feel of wind and rain often is!

Investigate the motion of tides. Record the sound of the sea running in and out on a beach.

Movement: Explore ways of moving forward and backward whilst on the spot. Try this standing, kneeling, sitting, and lying.

Observe waves breaking on the shore. Discover ways of moving in groups with successive flow through the group.

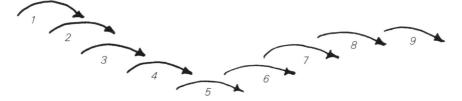

Observe, draw and photograph debris washed up on the shore.

Create group shapes to suggest damage and erosion. Make a sequence joining several shapes together with transitional movements to suggest the ebb and flow of the sea.

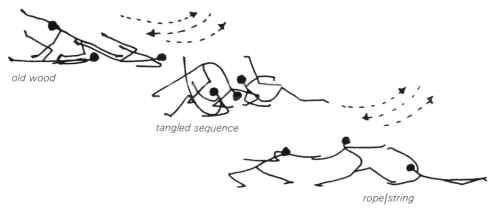

old wood

tangled sequence

rope/string

Observe and investigate plants and animals that depend on the tidal movement for life support.

Use group shapes to explore these opening and closing movements. Try to retain a constant if limited floor contact and some contact with each other so that the group is one. How far can the group extend, and in how many directions? Keep the movements smooth as if in water.

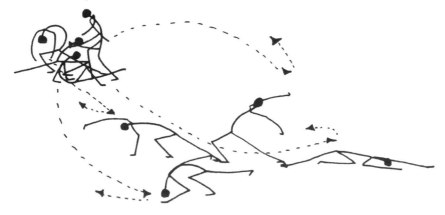

Watch and record waves and the way they move on shore or against rocks. Particularly note the successive flow and the power and try to capture this in movement. Explore successive flow through the body beginning at the top or the bottom, and repeat the ideas in small groups; gather the flow of movement so that it breaks or rolls over; use very slow motion to assist control.

Increase the size and distance travelled to suggest a storm. Consider climactic movement and its culmination ... decrease/freeze/break/dissolve.

Storm
Lightning: Light moves in straight lines and very fast — 186,000 miles per second.

Explore straight lines and sharp angles in ones or small groups.

Move from one formation to another very quickly. This will need practice to learn how to move economically and place the body accurately without correction. Some children find fast movement difficult; encourage them to simplify the shape of the body so that they can learn speed.

Use a cymbal as accompaniment.

Thunder: Use drums, sheets of metal or board to create the sound. Think of thunder as a rolling or rotating movement. Explore rolls across the class which are passed on from one person to another.

Wind: Rather than be the wind, think of wind as only evident by its effect on the environment. Observe clouds, grass, and washing. Observe litter being blown. Use a hair-dryer and bits of paper and empty tins to note and record movement. Let the body be blown about as litter, taking up distorted shapes to suggest damage. Look at the way litter accumulates in corners. Explore group shapes that gather together individuals.

Add sea, wind, lightning and thunder movements to create a storm at sea. Use voices calling for help or describing the storm.

Add music, for example the 'Storm' from Britten's *Peter Grimes*.

Always conclude with the end of the storm. Allow time for the children to become calm and still before leaving the lesson.

Lesson 50: The Carboniferous Period; Coal (7–13)

The formation of coal: Look at a piece of coal; feel its weight and texture. Coal is formed by land plants that decay in wet boggy conditions that limit the amount of oxygen admitted so that they decompose to form a carbon rich deposite.

The coal in this country was formed between 200 and 300 million years ago. The age of mammals is about 12 million years and the age of man 0.01 million years!

The land plants that formed coal were not the plants we know now. They were spore plants like giant horse tails and giant ferns. However, a fern plant will show the difference between coal and plants. Look at a fern; observe, feel and record its texture and structure.

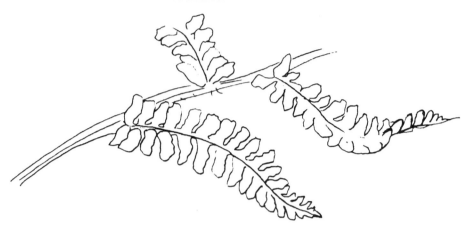

Movement: Capture the quality of the fern in body actions and shapes. Consider fragile, soft, limp, pliable, crushable, and spreading shapes.

Observe, draw, weigh and feel a lump of coal. Examine the structure, texture, fracture, shape, density and 'movement'. What does the coal tell you about the evolutionary process?

Movement: Capture the quality of the coal in body actions and shape. A group shape may be appropriate.

Compose a movement study that shows the transition from the fern state to the coal state.

Consider: individual to mass; separated to compressed; alive to 'dead'; soft to hard; young to old; flexible to rigid.

Perform the transition as if it takes a very long time. Use a drum beat to measure time. How long would this last if a drum beat represented ten years; a hundred years; a million years? How long is the dance study and what does the drum beat signify?

Repeat the study as if going back in time from coal to fern, that is, from now to the carboniferous time. Does this change the transitional movements?

Follow-up work

Find out about descent and modification in plants. Collect and investigate fossils.

Lesson 51: Migration; Why People Leave Home (8–13)

This lesson investigates the concept of why people move from one place to another. The understanding is illuminated by an historical example, The Great Migration. [Emigrants from the UK numbered one and a half million between 1850 and 1854.]

The purpose of the work is to empathize with migrants and the reasons for leaving home, and in particular to consider the decision to leave, the parting, and the journey.

Resources: Photocopies of archive material from the Ulster records office and from local record offices. Readings from documentary evidence such as diaries and letters can be used to accompany and support understanding within practical interpretation.

Movement: The following dance ideas can be used in isolation or as part of an inter-media project.

1. Reasons for leaving

Consider and discuss famine; poverty; unemployment; increase in population; mechanization; punishment; the effect of a class system; adventure. Look at paintings of the period.

Create a group image like a still photograph which clearly shows the characters and their story.

famine, poverty

convicts

Observe a group image and imagine an individual's thoughts. What is the person feeling, thinking, saying? Write some of these thoughts and feelings down. The writing can be used to accompany the 'photograph', spoken by the characters, or developed as a piece of prose.

Using these thoughts, work on the group image and clarify the gestures, levels, relationship and grouping. Think about the shape of the bodies rather than mimed gestures.

2. Social dependency and interrelationship

Explore movement as a symbolic expression of this dependency.

In twos, explore physical bodily support.

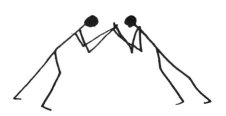

Whilst taking care of your partner find out what happens if one person removes the support ... fall, crumble, collapse, stand alone. Use one of these ideas in slow motion to create a dance image expressing the withdrawal of support.

3. Sheltering and being sheltered

Make a body position that embraces a space, protects it and shelters it. In twos, combine a position of being enclosed and enclosing.

Remove the protector — what happens to the partner? Does he collapse, flee, become strong?

Remove the protected — what happens to the protector when the reason for protecting no longer applies?

Use these ideas to create a motif; polish and refine, removing any unnecessary movements. It will probably help to move in slow motion.

4. The moment of parting: sensitivity and dynamics

Individually explore the interaction of both hands ... holding, resting, sliding through ... very, very slowly, bring hands almost to the point of separation ... and separate ... emphasize the moment with suddenness as if snapping or breaking the link.

Repeat this exercise with the hand of a partner.

Repeat allowing the body to echo the movement of the hands. If necessary add stepping, change of level or weight support.

This movement idea can be incorporated in the group 'photograph' so that characters move according to their chosen role.

Discuss the interaction between members of a family group. Children may implicitly use their own personal experience as reference.

5. Packing: concentration and imagination

Imagine packing personal belongings in a chest knowing that they will not be seen again for some time. Leave room for a very special article and pack this last of all; imagine the memories associated with this object. Finally close the lid. The following excerpt might accompany this activity, individuals repeating the words as if checking the list.

The following is the lowest outfit recommended to Parishes for their Laborers.

A Fur Cap.	Two Jersey Frocks.
A warm great Coat.	Four Shirts.
A Flushing Jacket and Trowsers.	Four pairs Stockings.
A Duck Frock and Trowsers.	Three pairs Shoes.
A canvas Frock & two pairs of Trowsers	A Bible and Prayer Book.

Women in the same proportion, especially a warm Cloak.

All the above may be purchased at Petworth.

It is also a matter of great importance, that Emigrants should take with them a good Character, (if they should have the happiness to possess one,) fairly written and well attested, also Copies of Marriage or Baptismal Registers, or any other Certificates or Papers likely to be useful; the whole to be inclosed in a small Tin Case.

———

J. Phillips, Printer, Petworth.

6. Embarkation: the ship

Add information about sailing ships, the means of navigation, and the length of the journey. Imagine families sharing cramped quarters for many weeks. Imagine the necessary cooperation and the sense of community.

Using a large amount of space, move as if spreading bedding and shaking pillows before lying down to sleep. Repeat the same activity but sharing a small space with many others. Express courtesy and cooperation by helping and apologizing. Gradually settle down to rest and stillness, if necessary using someone else as a pillow or as support. This activity requires sensitivity and may develop from trust exercises (see also Lessons 12 and 13).

Whilst lying still — however uncomfortable — imagine the expanse of the sea outside the ship. This represents 3000 or more miles that are dangerous and unknown, and symbolizes the future for the emigrants. Slowly turn the eyes and then the head to focus on the outside space beyond even the limit of the hall or classroom. Follow that focus and so move carefully out of the group, standing with the back to the centre looking outward and beyond.

The outside space can be defined by chairs, the back of the chair representing the deck rail of the ship. Allow the whole body posture to express the anticipation of the future in both time and space.

7. The ship at sea

All stand, generally spaced out but facing in the same direction. Follow a swaying motion of the front person to suggest the roll of the ship at sea. Keep this movement slow and constant, almost hypnotic. Write some words to express the thoughts, hopes and fears about the new land and use some of these words to accompany the swaying motion. Interupt this motion with the cry of 'land!' and freeze sharing a common focus of sighted land.

8. Arrival
Using resource material, write a letter or part letter home to describe an event. Group these events to create a final still photograph such as could be sent home, each character reading extracts from the letter according to character.

Follow-up work
Music: create sound to accompany the motion of the sea. Compose a ballad about the journey.

Written work: as already described, write letters; make posters to persuade people to go to the new world. List arrangements for departure, and plan timetables and lists of stores.

Drama: explore life before the departure, and dramatize events that precipitate the decision to leave home.

Discussion: personal and family experiences; local history.

5
A Glossary of Dance Terms With Teaching Ideas

Abstraction

The art activity, whatever the form, is about focusing on a particular event, idea, or thing, and distancing it from actual reality so that it can be freely considered. This focus and distance is abstraction from reality. Children making dance, drama, music, or pictures are engaged in identifying and selecting relevant and logical ideas. They are abstracting and putting into abstract form something that has, or is given, significance.

Action

Action describes what the body is doing. The clue to thinking about action is to use verbs. Some verbs, such as jump, walk, run, and sit, are particularly associated with human movement. Other associations will extend the vocabulary of movement, for example:

Machinery: thrust, hammer, glide, hoist.
Plant life: grow, sway, disperse, enfold, wither.
Insects: hover, dart, swarm, alight, scuttle.
Clouds: pile up, scud, accumulate, drift.
Mud: ooze, squelch, stick, squeeze, splash.
Roget's Thesaurus is a very comprehensive source — see 'motion'.

Action activities

It is very helpful to have emotive action words ready so that moving 'in a different way' is positively suggested. Children like words and respond well to words that also suggest feelings and situations, such as deviate, distort, depress, invade, grapple, or struggle. Explore different words that have similar meanings. Stillness, for example, might be danced as rest, stagnation, immobilized, switched off, asleep, dead, waiting.

Add action words together to make a movement sequence. Select actions that are compatible, opposite, similar. Perform an action with changes in speed, level, place, body part, size, number of dancers.

Find the rhythm of an action sequence; change the rhythm.

Use a given sequence and compare individual performance. This can be very exciting in a class of different ethnic origins.

Create a dance composition using variations on the action theme; add music; bring different group studies together; put into a context; perform in a dance style: dramatic, jazzy, blues, comic, ballroom.

Consider related actions such as:

- actions of the face — smile, frown, stare, avert, face.
- actions associated with secrecy — creep, slink, sidle.
- actions in mountainous country — trudge, climb, haul, traverse, clamber, tumble.
- actions of retreat — withdraw, shrink back, flee, escape.

Consider the action of things seen and felt:

- move like things blown by the wind — swirl, flap, wave.
- move like thunder sounds — roll, clash, crash.
- move like water — ripple, flow, reflect, pour, drip.

Find actions suggested by sound, colour, texture:

- the sound of a cymbal
- the feel of velvet
- the look of barbed wire
- the response to black.

Action and Shape

Shape is a consequence of action. Consider the shape of a pushing hand; a ripple through the body; an advancing group.

What is the shape of a dispersing group, of a crushed trio, of a soaring reach? Stop the action as if in a still photograph and study the shape. Use a change of shape to suggest the next action.

Actions Defined

V. Preston Dunlop categorizes five activities:

(i) **Gesture**: Any movement that is not concerned with supporting the body. The hand gestures used in conversation provide examples which can be performed by other body parts as with the pointing foot or a knee that is protective.

(ii) A **step** transfers weight from one foot to the other. In dance weight can be transferred step-like from any body part, e.g. foot to hands, bottom to shoulder.

(iii) **Travel**: Any movement used to get from one place to another: walk, run, and leap are obvious examples. Travel also includes actions such as roll, wriggle, slide, fall.

Dramatic qualities can be added to travel actions such as trudge, loiter, stagger, scamper, gallop, bound.

Do not be confused that stepping and travel overlap.

(iv) **Flight**: The body off the ground and in the air, thus jump, leap, hop, dive.

Jumps use the feet to take off and land; feet can jump from one to one, one to two, two to two, one to the same, or one to the other.

(v) **Turning**: Any movement that changes front including isolated body parts. The whole body can move in quarter or half turns standing or rolling. Isolated body parts such as the head, hand or rib cage can roll, twist and turn. The term also includes groups of dancers turning.

Interaction

Action and interaction is the way an action is answered or promotes a response, leads into another action, or is the result of another action. Interaction can be between one's own movements or include that of other dancers. It may be spontaneous or choreographed. Interaction is being sensitive and involved.

Try a single action that passes from one to another: running a relay race is an example. The action can be started by one and finished or modified by another. A sequence such as sink, rise, freeze, melt, can pass from one group to another as it changes or during the change.

Action is a dance building block: ideas, feelings, and patterns have to be expressed in action. A good question to ask of a planned lesson 'what actions are the children actually going to do?'
see Lessons 23, 24, 25, 26, 39, 47, 48, 49, and 50.

Affinity

The logical relationship between movements and what they express. When we see a movement we see expression and we are able to recognize inappropriate movements or movements that seem illogical. Affinity between movement and expression is 'picked up' through the experience of both feeling and observing feeling — it is learnt in context.

The kind of movement thirty children might choose to use to express, say, 'awakening', or 'suddenly coming to a decision', or 'disappointment', will have something in common however varied the movements.

Laban's analysis of movement sought to identify some of these affinities, for example, a flow of movement that is bound and restricted will maintain balance, retain body shape, move directly to a destination, and adhere to a constant pattern or idea. This analysis also includes 'effort attitudes' in which motion factors are identified with particular emotions. Thus weight and flow qualities are identified with a dream-like feeling and little awareness of the material world.
See Chapter 16 in Dunlop (1963).

Beginning and End

These are probably the most important moments in a movement sequence or dance composition, and must be clearly differentiated from the everyday movement that precedes or follows the dance even in the classroom lesson. 'Find a starting place' or 'hold the finishing position' means establishing the time and space 'frame' of the dance.

Children – and dancers – need time to think themselves into their art form. This is also true for the spectator in the theatre, and the lowering of lights and rising of the curtain serve this purpose. In the classroom lights and curtains are replaced by time to concentrate, possibly with stillness and silence, or music and imagery. It is essential that children are given time to believe in their bodily movement and its expression.

Body Awareness

The ability to sense where out bodies are and where parts are in relation to other parts. With closed eyes, hold out an arm at full length on a level with nose and then your eyes. The position of the arm is fairly accurate. This uses the sense of knowing where the body is, without which we would be unable use our bodies at all – the KINESTHETIC SENSE. A professional dancer develops this sense to perform very complex movements in quick succession.

Body Sensing

Lie on the floor in any position, close the eyes and listen to any sounds; change listening to body sensing; feel the difference between parts that touch the ground, touch each other or touch nothing. Feel differences in pressure, temperature, texture, and softness. Some parts may even be in pain! Concentrate on different parts: try to locate the back of the knee, the bottom of the spine, or the top of the head. Change the position of the body to feel different parts. Such sensing is not physically active but is a necessary dance quality. It takes time to do and time to establish as a way of working.

Figure 27   Sensing where body parts are in relation to other parts of the body.

Sensing can also be explored whilst standing, kneeling, resting, or leaning against a wall. Support each other's weight, make combined shapes, and be aware of body contact.

Body Part Awareness

Awareness includes awareness of touch; weight; body weight support; parts moving; parts that initiate movement or complete a movement; parts that are emphasized; parts that lead or follow.

Activity: Touching Body Parts

Touch the floor with different parts in succession: tap the floor with nose, forehead, fingers, heels. Tap the floor to a rhythmic pattern: ////,////,////. Tap shoulders ////, noses ////, hips ////, knees ////, elbows ////, palms ////, ear ////, and so on. Vary the rhythm and the down-beat. Use music, percussion or voice. Give sufficient repetition for everyone to catch up.

This is a fun warm-up, especially if body parts are switched so that bottom follows tummy then noses and toes. Touch fingers to knees, ear to shoulder, forehead to knees. Allow for invention and more flexible bodies than your

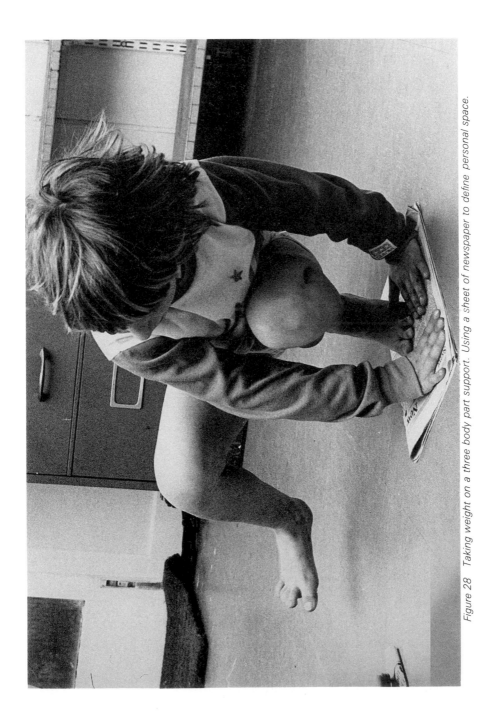

Figure 28 Taking weight on a three body part support. Using a sheet of newspaper to define personal space.

own! Vary the timing and the phrase. For example, bring fingers to the knees very quickly then slowly separate them.

Body Support: Using the Floor

The most impressive characteristic of classical ballet is the way in which the body is carried and balanced on the feet, and this can be a discouraging image for older children. Use the floor to get rid of problems like balancing or falling. The floor is safe, concrete, permanent, and a less conspicuous place to be than upright.

The Management of Body Weight

Make body contact with the floor, as much or as little as possible; take weight on two, three, or four parts; take weight on unusual parts; change parts as quickly or as slowly as possible. Make a sequence using a changed weight support. Move from the spot keeping one bit stuck to the floor. Supported on one body part, change shape to high, wide, thin, jagged; retain shape whilst resting on different parts. Work in twos and small groups to match or share weight support. Add change in levels, size, speed, and proximity. Work on transitions.

Useful imagery —seaweed, water plants, creepers.

Task: create a sequence which includes movement in three different directions, each initiated by a different body part. Repeat and vary the speed and phrasing. See also Lessons 1, 2 and 3.

The Actual Weight of the Body and the Management of Body Weight

Lie on the floor and relax by easing the tension in each body part. Be aware of the feel of the body pressing on the floor. As you breathe in and out, feel the energy of the body flow from the centre out through the fingers, the toes and the top of the head.

Gently lift and lower the leg or arm of a partner and feel the weight. Find the actual weight of the body, calculate the weight of different parts, and lift equivalent weights.

In fours or sixes, lift a rigid or relaxed body and note the difference.

Lift an arm and let it fall loosely, notice any swing and how the arm comes to rest. Repeat with both arms, a leg, the torso, the whole upper body.

Stay near the floor and explore the freedom of giving in to body weight by rolling, sitting, falling, kneeling, overbalancing, crouching.

Support the weight on different body parts to find possible actions. What kind of action changes the weight support?

219

The Head

The head is heavy in proportion to its size, and its position at the top of the body affects balance and mobility.

Retain foot contact with the floor and move the head. Aim for mobility and change of body shape.

Use the weight of the head to drop the top of the body and lift with the top of the head.

Make a head mask with antennae and wear it to accentuate the movement of the head.

Share a large face mask and move as one body. Travel, turn, and change level without 'losing face'.

Eyes and Focus

See Lessons 32 and 33.

Ears and Listening

Some children have limited opportunity to really concentrate on the quality of sound or of silence, and noisy children are sometimes so because the environment or the teacher is noisy. Provide opportunity for the children to practise focused listening. Use different sound qualities to accompany or stimulate movement. See also Lesson 34.

Use the ear to lead bodily movements as if listening to locations around the body or in the general space.

The Nose

The nose sticks out and often adds humour to movement. Lead with the nose to travel or change the shape of the body. Let the nose arrive first or last and explore the effect. Discover movements that are best led by the nose – or the chin, forehead, or top of the head.

Shoulders

Shoulders are frequently tense and hunched with anxiety or lack or confidence. Lift, drop, rotate and wriggle the shoulders to relax them, both separately and together. Explore the rotation of the arms in relation to the rotation of the shoulders. Move the shoulders to express protection, shutting out others, alarm, giving up. Use a shoulder movement to initiate an opening and closing arm gesture.

Fingers and Hands

Fingers and hands are flexible and can move when the rest of the body is still. They can be used to make dance in the classroom and introduce movement ideas in a 'safe' way.

Open and close fingers slowly, suddenly, successively, simultaneously, jerkily, smoothly, as much or as little as possible.

Shake hands loosely, let them drip off the end of the wrists, throw them, fling them, catch them. Move them high, low, near, and far from the body.

Use hands to collect, hold, deposit, grab. Pick up something that is precious, fragile, slimy, alive.

Screw up a piece of paper and handle it as if it is a broken bird, pass it to a partner, protect it from others or from wind and rain.

Holding hands is a natural way of making body contact with others. Use four hands to explore the pattern and shape that they make. Play the 'one potato, two potato' game or the 'stone, scissors, paper' game.

Join two hands and play hide and seek with the two free hands.

Follow a lead hand and swop leader.

Figure 29   Interpreting the structure of plants. Fingers and hands are flexible and can be used to make dance when space is limited.

221

Make up hand dances to accompany songs and stories. Use hand percussion sounds to make a sound story.

Explore hand gestures: point, press, stroke, snatch. Find appropriate placing and timing. Join with a partner to match or contrast the actions. Emphasize the hands by wearing gloves or paint.

Consider the structure of the hands and the action when using the side, palm, knuckle, back, one finger. Explore the different moods of these actions and combine them to make an expressive sequence.

Explore the rotation of each hand and its flexibility, change the quality of movement and retain continuity. Use change of speed and action to accompany music.

Create a pattern of movement with one hand, pass it and catch it with the other. Imagine the movement can be thrown into space, chase it and capture it. Dance it with both hands and throw the pattern to a partner.

Place hands in different places: high, low, in front, behind, far apart, together; hide them sit or stand on them, walk on them, travel with hands arriving first. Make silhouettes on a wall or screen. Make a dance with no hands or only using hands.

Feet

The line of the upright body is affected by the way the weight is supported on the feet. Weight should fall equally on three 'pads', the heel and the metatarsals of the big and little toe. The way the feet are placed on the floor in walking changes the posture and the character of the body. Try walking with the weight falling on the heel, toe, inside, and outside,

Feet can turn in or out; steps can be wide, in a line, small, large, uneven.

With the weight on or off the feet, they can prod, kick, rotate, flex, press, push, stamp, curl, point. Spread and wriggle the toes. Take weight on the feet as if the floor is hot, sticky, slippery, bumpy. Travel using different foot parts to make a rhythm: toe; heel; inside, outside.

Step as if the big toe is an eye searching for a good resting place ... and makes a mistake!

Knees

The structure of the knee can easily by damaged by the sudden support of body weight or violent deep knee bends. Take-off and landing should cushion weight-taking and falls practised to avoid using the knee.

Like the nose, knees can stick out and the knees make a difference to character of movement. Bend the knees to make them very evident and travel or turn with knees leading. Travel alternating steps with no knees and steps with knees emphasized.

Elbows

The use of the elbow extends the mobility of the arm and the shaping of movements. Explore the rotation of the arm using the shoulder and the elbow allowing the elbow to lead the movement. Draw circles and figures-of-eight crossing the body and changing level. Move the elbow around the body so that the body is forced to follow. Lead first with one elbow and then the other.

The Chest

The chest is the centre of levity and effects the sense and management of lift and weightlessness. The openness of the chest contributes to performance projection and efficient breathing.

The Body Centre

Control of the body centre uses the big muscles to carry the weight of the body allowing the arms and legs to move freely. This control also contributes to the stability and balance of the body, and to the full projection of movement. There should be the sense of energy going out from the centre and recovery as if energy is gathered to the centre.

The technique of body centre contract and release was developed by Martha Graham and is the basis of her dance style.

Choreutics

The study of spatial form, a system devised by Laban in which the organization of the kinesphere is related to the 'import' of the dance. The spatial elements include the location, direction, shape, and distance from the centre of the body. (See *Choreutics* by R. Laban, edited by L. Ullmann, 1966.)

Choreography

The process of selecting and forming movement into a dance form. It involves designing the action; creating the dance with a conscious intent to say something; composing the form; developing appropriate techniques; presentation with attention to the rapport between the choreographer's plan and the way the audience perceive the dance.

The term is sometimes reserved for the professional theatre. Whether children create, make, compose, or choreograph dance is immaterial as long as their dance experience includes dance-making.

Composition

The way the dance is put together to make a whole work. It includes putting together movements, phrases, ideas, dancers, and music.

Formal composition makes use of established forms and can sometimes stimulate ideas and invention. For example: theme and variation, rondo, canon, suite. A useful form for young children is an ABA form or variations such as ABAB, ABCDA, or ABACA.

An ABA form can make use of an idea contributed by each partner, or by two groups.

Dance steps

The transition of weight from one foot to the other −on the ground or with flight. Examples are:

Skip −a step, hop.

Gallop −a step, leap.

Polka −step, step, step, hop

Pavane −a slow step in duple time.

Waltz − a step in triple time using the rhythm of a swing, strong/weak/weak.

March −regular stepping, usually four beats to a measure. In the British army a slow march is 75 steps per minute, a quick march is 108 steps per minute.

Minuet −a step in triple time which includes a leg gesture.
(See *May I Have The Pleasure* by Quirey, Bradshaw, and Smedley, published by the BBC in 1976, with video.)

Improvisation with accompanying sound is preferred to conscious counting and stepping. Stepping to singing is a natural way in, 'row, row, row the boat' is an example that includes three different step patterns.

Distortion

A change or modification of the natural condition. A gesture can be distorted by a change in shape; size; force; speed; body part; level; rhythm.

Drama

Drama is about people and their experiences, who they are and what they do. As in dance, drama organizes space and time, but space is identifiable place, and time is organized by events, by acts that 'spring from the past are directed towards the future' (Langer, 1957).

Drama essentially deals with commitments and consequences. It is about space, time, and people.

Dance – Drama

This is neither dance nor drama but a form of its own. It brings together the spatial/temporal design of dance and the acts of people. The effect is to give a kind of distancing to characters and situations, and to colour the design with the past history and future destiny of characters.

Dramatic Movement

Movements or dance are described as dramatic when qualities such as force and speed are emphasized and so can be identified with life events. For example,

- gestures that are strong and sudden appear angry ... angry about something;
- relationships that come to a climax;
- shapes and pathways that create a tension.

To say dance is not dramatic might mean that it has a different style, that it is pure design, or that it is music-like in its shape and phrasing. It might also mean that the dance is lacking in vitality.

Dynamics

A general term to describe the way a movement can be performed, using change in (i) force, (ii) speed, and (iii) continuity.

There is a variety of terms used to describe these qualities such as (i) forcefulness, weight, strength, (ii) time, speed, and (iii) progression, continuity, flow. Dynamic qualities may also include the spatial pathway of a movement (see Space).

Similar dynamic changes occur in spoken language and change in stress on words contributes to a change in the meaning. Thus: 'I *would* like you to come with me' spoken as a gentle invitation, or 'I would like *you* to come with me' spoken with the force of a command.

The meaning of a movement is altered when the dynamic qualities are changed. Indeed it is the dynamic qualities that contribute most to meaning in movement. Intentions and attitudes colour the way we move and speak, so that we learn to use and interpret the dynamics of speech and body movement as we acquire the means of communication. We know what it is to be in a dreadful hurry and we recognize that feeling when we see someone moving very quickly.

The investigation and performance of different dynamic qualities in the dance lesson serve several purposes: (i) the manipulation of these qualities enables the dancer to examine and clearly communicate a range of feelings and ideas including very subtle variations (ii) the development of an individual movement personality thus a child who freely rushes headlong into any activity can be encouraged to experience and sense the quality of calm and stillness. (iii) the awareness of similar qualities in the environment.

The aim of the dance syllabus is to provide for a full range of movement qualities that can be appropriately selected, performed, and read, with clarity and understanding.

All movements have force, speed, and flow qualities, but not all movements are clearly expressive. To understand this, imagine a horizontal line, A–B, on which A and B represent the maximum and minimum conditions possible. The centre of the line represents a condition that exists but is negligible. It is only the notable and emphasized dynamic qualities that contribute to meaning.

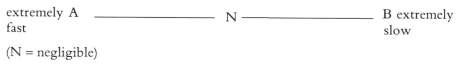

extremely A ————————— N ————————— B extremely
fast   slow

(N = negligible)

Time

This is possibly the easiest dynamic quality to explore and perform, and is also an aid in classroom control and management. It is about moving very fast or very slowly and all the degrees of speed between the two. Change in time can accelerate or decelerate, and contribute surprise, climax, hesitation, reluctance, anticipation. Little change in time is likely to be monotonous.

Activity:
Travel as fast as possible in a varied pathway. Travel as slowly as possible. Remain absolutely still. Combine these as individual sequences. Move fast between still bodies or travel slowly while others rush past. Discover the difference when performing a similar sequence as a group. Perform any movement, finish the movement suddenly or gradually decrease the speed. Work in twos to create a question and answer sequence and discover speed qualities that suggest opposition, agreement, agitation, tranquillity. Speed affects the atmosphere: fast movement is noisy, fun, careless, and uncontrolled; slow movement is calm, quiet, controlled, and introspective. Contrast these two atmospheres, moving from one to the other, so that uncontrolled movement suddenly comes under control.

Experiment with speed in the classroom using normal activities such as entering the classroom, calling the register, or changing for PE. Discuss the mood and compare different speeds of actions at work, play, in sport, at home.

Record, compare and experiment to find appropriate speed qualities. Look at speed and function in the in the natural world, for example, clouds forming, plants unfolding, insects moving. Look at videos about the natural world which include slowed-down bird flight or speeded-up plant growth.

The sustained breath rhythm

Sit or lie, concentrate on the rise and fall of breathing. Gradually move the body in time to this rhythm, adding rocking, rising, standing, and walking. Discuss the mood and the control of the body.

The speed of the pulse

Repeat the above activity using a pulse beat. Add a drum or voice. Compare the mood and control with that of the breath rhythm.

Introduce notation symbols used in music and Labanotation (See Notation). Use these symbols to record, observe, and perform movement, and to create movement sequences.

Explore increase of speed and ways of resolving such speed. Listen to climax in music and in a story. Look at climax in visual art. Sense a climax in a whole class activity. Children love clapping faster and faster, but can they find the point of no return and reach a common conclusion?

Watch a screwed-up plastic bag unfold. Very little needs to be said — the movement is dramatic and clearly illustrates speed and shaping. Perform the same movement with the body, beginning with a crumpled-up position. Reverse to shrink the body shape.

Combine changes of speed with other activities. For example, in a sequence of making three body shapes, use a different speed for each transition. Experiment to find the most exciting or the most appropriate time. Which shapes are best made slowly? What happens to curves that are danced very quickly?

Perform a dance motif three times, each at a different speed. How is the action and the meaning changed?

Combine different speeds using different dancers or different body parts: make sudden movements with the hands whilst stepping slowly, move as a group but combine sudden moving dancers with very slow ones. Gradually increase or decrease the speed to change roles.

Force/Weight/Power/Strength

Force describes the amount of energy used to perform an action, or the amount of force that appears to be used. The two are not synonymous. In classical ballet much energy is used to create the illusion of weightlessness. In dance literature the variety of words used to describe force can be confusing. Generally the following mean the same:

Force, strong, weight, with gravity, power, intense.
Heavy, giving way to gravity, relaxed, yielding.
Light, weightless, against gravity, fine touch.

There is a difference between pushing against the actual weight of an object and moving as if pushing, although the real experience of pushing against real resistance does help to achieve the bodily feel of force.

Yielding to force, including yielding to gravity, produces heaviness in which the body has weight but lacks strength. Relaxation of the body can be used to develop bodily awareness; to prepare for or recover from action; to loosen supported body parts such as shoulders and hands; to express yielding ideas such as melting and falling; in trust activities.

Lightness or lack or force is more abstract movement concept and more to do with an attitude or feeling for lightness. It is often more difficult for boys, weightlessness being less evident in traditional male behaviour, and concrete images and examples are very necessary.

Activity
Use the floor to stamp, press, push and bang: the floor provides actual resistance. Repeat similar actions in the space around the body, imagining that there is something to move against. Any strong movement that uses the total reach loses its strength both visually and physically — strong actions must show resistance and suggest that there is yet more strength to follow!

Combine stamp, kick, swipe, lunge, punch, thrust, throw. Find the most appropriate body part and explore the actions with other body parts.

Plan the location of selected actions: kick, stamp, throw; above, below, to the side, behind, across. Perform the sequence twice, using sudden then slow movements. Add a rhythm. Work with a partner and use the movements as if in conversation.

Use force to push or pull a partner, use backs, bottoms, hands, sides; make allowances for unequal strength. Repeat but imagine a partner. Discuss the difference, and perform the movements to make the imagined partner 'visible'.

As a group move with resistance or against resistance introduce travel, levels, different speeds. Add situation or emotional conditions.

Combine these qualities using sudden or gradual transitions: a movement that is forceful and increases in speed; travel with interrupted flow and sudden bursts of activity; a slow gesture that finishes with a strong accent.
See Lessons 14, 15, 18, 23, and 48.

Continuity

Dance progresses through time and space, using the flow or continuity of movement without which there is no dance.

The progression of movement means that shapes and relationships are seen becoming; rising high or sinking low; a closed-in body shape closes in from wherever it was before. As dance images come and go so they express the way ideas, feelings, and experiences come and go and the changes that take place so that transitions or changes take place because dance progresses, and changes can take place in different ways: a speedy change is different from a sustained change, a restrained move forward is different from a willing advance.

The flow of a movement can be free and open or restricted and tight — the flow affects the way the movement progresses. The first creates a fluid continuous feeling, the second is likely to be hesitant with abrupt breaks in the continuity. Young children often find it easy to move freely because they have little fear of falling and are in touch with the spontaneous movement of their bodies. Conscious movement control and theoretical application often inhibits this freedom but it may be recaptured through increased skill and confidence in both ideas and body management.

Activity
Free movement needs sufficient space for whole body movement and to allow movement in any direction such as rolling forward, turning round, sliding across, falling down, swinging up, and running around.

Anticipate hazards and plan a way of stopping to maintain some control. Make more space by using small groups at a time; achieve some self-control by moving freely in between still bodies and define the duration of movement.

Play 'tag' in twos, repeat with imaginary partners. Whirl round holding a partner's hand, change level and speed, in slower motion spin off and follow the action of the body, allow the motion to gradually cease. Use agility mattresses for leaping and landing, and take advantage of swimming lessons to explore freedom in the water. Do not confuse confidence with carelessness.

Use streamers of crêpe paper to extend the free movement or arm and hand gestures; use long full skirts, loose material, loose hair. Move to free, happy music using the volume control to increase activity and bring it to stillness. Use swinging actions to explore the use of gravity, take swings into jumps and turns, and allow the weight of the body to determine its pathway and action.

Controlled movement restrains the freedom and the dancer or circumstance determines the movement rather than the movement itself; continuity is interrupted and pathways become precise and action tense. Move as if carrying something fragile: eggs on the head; a time bomb; a damaged bird. Make a movement phrase that stops at specified moments using a count or sound accompaniment. Perform a movement as if in a strobe light or early silent movie. Try robot-like or machine-like movements. Create a movement sequence combining different actions: step/turn/lie/roll/stand/travel. Perform the sequence with continous flow. Draw the pattern of the movement and add pauses; dance the notatted pattern with accuracy.

Progression is also structured by the compositional form of the dance, a dance image may change within a succession of repeated phrases or a set of variations based on a motif. Indeed all the elements of the dance media effect the flow of the dance: dynamics, technique, action, composition, use of space, phrasing and rhythm.

Editing and Polishing

Refining a piece of work and preparing a dance for performance.

Editing: Dances are often too long. Erase unnecessary movements and ideas including those that might be very exciting but do not belong to the piece.

Heighten moments of most significance, and consider their contribution and placing within the whole composition.

Check the logical order. Sometimes the end is really the starting point, or two middle sections are the wrong way round.

Check that the end is a conclusion and that the audience are not waiting for more to come or have to be told to applaud!

Polishing: Check body management and practice or modify movements that lack skill. Heighten interest by clarifying or exaggerating the dynamic qualities. Check on 'fudgy' transitions, sharpen contrasts, smooth fluent passages. Identify exit and entrance places. Sometimes a dance can be improved by using much less space. Experiment with alternative possibilities taking it in turns to watch the result.

Do not be too explicit. Make the audience work, but with understanding, not confusion.

Give some thought to the title. A title can cue the spectator in to an appropriate way of looking or can mislead. Maybe the piece needs a title that gives no clue.

Attend to sound. Either use live sound, silence, or reproduced sound that is as perfectly reproduced as possible.

Effort

The term used by Laban to describe action in movement which includes the attitude or feeling that 'colours' the action and produces the quality of movement. Attitudes produce movement qualities and movement qualities produce attitudes. In Laban's movement analysis the four motion factors of effort — weight, time, space, and flow — are related to sensing, feeling, intuition, and thinking.

Improvisation

The immediate movement response to an idea or stimulus. This is often the most profound and sensitive response as the body is most in touch with the feel of the idea. Improvisation can be used in composition but it is sometimes difficult to recall the movement ideas. Free movement response to music can be an enjoyable but empty activity.

The level of improvisation is directly related to the level of skill and extent of vocabulary as well as imagination. The ability to improvise is developed by working within a given framework or answering a task. For example:

Use the rhythm of the music to travel across the floor for sixteen bars.

Use paper streamers to create continuous patterns around the body.

Travel as if the floor is sticky, bumpy, slimy, prickly, muddy, icy, hot.

Respond to words, pictures, the shape and texture of objects. Make a sequence using three words: jab, twist, open; hover, dart, fall; sea, sky, field.

Improvise to a partner's percussion sound. Respond to the change in mood.

Improvise hand movements as if exploring underground, add a verbal commentary. Move to a partner's commentary.

In fours, build a sequence of movement by each adding a gesture. Illustrate a different theme for each round: anger, waiting, authority, bird, wind.

Jumping

See under Action

Lyrical Dance

A general term which usually describes dance in which the melodic and song-like phrasing of movement is more important than the design or drama. Lyrical dance is frequently accompanied by music of similar quality. In school dance such movement really needs music to sustain the ease and mood of the movement, plus skilful foot-work and fine phrasing.

Media

The materials of dance. This is what dance is actually made of, in the way that music is made of sound and duration, and a drawing is made of marks and spaces. The materials are the body, the actions, the space, and time. Ancillary materials might also be used, such as costume, music, speech, props, scenery, lighting, and film.

When planning a lesson it is necessary to consider the kind of materials that the children are likely to use to explore and express any content. The level of skill in body management and awareness of the way space is shaped contribute to the way ideas are explored and shared. Similarly the exploration of ideas carries with it the developing ability to dance.

Mime

A very sophisticated and technical art form. The body moves to create the illusion of reality, thus a man miming taking a bath makes the spectator see the taps and the level of the bath water. The technical difficulty lies in managing the body with converse gravity, so that the strength to float must look weightless, a body in fine balance must look as if it is supported by an imaginary wall.

Mime in school dance is unlikely to use such a developed art form, but mimed actions can support, stimulate and develop dance ideas. To imagine moving in a high wind or to use the hands as if holding something precious is a way of finding the appropriate gestures and dynamic qualities.

Motif

A brief and self-existent phrase of movement that can be developed.

A movement motif is a useful way into dance composition. The idea may derive from a variety of starting points:

- location and action.........travel, lift, turn, extend.
- observation of ice melting..............sharp, hard, still, soften, melt, move downward, lie.
- gestures.................offer, take, posses, share.
- relationship...........the floor, the wall, a person.

Motivation

That which excites us to work with enthusiasm. It differs for each individual and may be to do with need, expectancy of certain results, or need for change. There is also the motivation to create, do make something where there was nothing before. This is the motivation to conceive a dance which also determines its form and excites the energy and imagination to realise that form. Each dance lesson needs its motivation. It is about finding the key or the way into the activity and its significance.

To motivate the children the teacher must know something of their interests and their environment so that the dance lesson is relevant to life outside the school or injects something new and startling. Find something that makes the children curious: a parcel, a new way of looking at the view from the window, something to do with body language and relationships, body image and fitness, watching adults, real sensory experience like standing in the rain or being blown by the wind. Let them share laughter by looking at something funny or doing funny movement. Enable them to wonder at their achievement and give them the confidence to share their ideas and invention.

Motivation for a Dance Work

That which stimulates the creation of a dance. This differs for each artist and often for each creation. It includes the desire to give form to an idea; experimenting with the bodily skill and ideas contributed by dancers; an idea that is lyrical, narrative, or pure design; wanting to create dance; fulfilling a commission.

Movement

Simultaneous Movement

Movement happening at the same time, in which whole body, whole group, or whole class move at once. The movement can be slow or sudden: thus a group can move from A to B in one unified movement or in several simultaneous moves.

Combinations of successive and simultaneous movements in study lead to ideas that echo, arrive at the same time, finish one after the other, overtake, suddenly stop and then add an afterthought, grow as one and decrease in size bit by bit.

Successive Movement

One thing following another. One movement, one body part, a movement that travels from head to toe, one member of a group. Thus a movement can pass through the body or through a group. Movement can also be passed from one group to another and appear to travel in the space between. As it passes movement can develop, change, add something, or take something away, and a group can become successively larger or smaller.

Notation

In mathematics and language we accept it as normal that we are able to use written symbols to represent meaning. These symbols enable us to manipulate and create ideas and to record our observations and activities.

A published system of dance notation is a recent invention. In the past classical ballets relied on eye-witness accounts to keep a dance in the repertory, and many dances both of the theatre and of the people have been lost. Notation is now available and dance companies employ librarians to make and store dance scores which contain collections of ballets, folk, national and ethnic dance. Notation is also in movement therapy to provide diagnostic and treatment records.

All those who create dance, whether in school or in the theatre, use some method of writing dance even if it is a personal collection of squiggles and pinmen. It may not be necessary to replace this personal method, but a knowledge of a notation system can extend one's own dance thinking and make it possible for others to read the dance.

There are two currently used notation systems.

Choreology was devised and developed by Rudolph and Joan Benesh in the early 1950s. This system uses the five lines of the music stave within a square to represent the span of the arms and the height of the body.

Head

Shoulder

Waist

Knee

Floor

The dynamic symbols are also taken from music: ppp means completely relaxed and ff means very strong. (See *An Introduction to Benesh Dance Notation*, published by A. and C. Black Ltd. in 1956.)

Labanotation was devised by Rudolph Laban, also around the early 1950s. This system shows which part of the body is being used, the spatial location, and the dynamic quality. Thus:

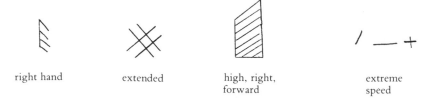

right hand   extended   high, right,   extreme
                                                          forward   speed

The notation system is very comprehensive and can record any movement. It also uses a stave so that sound accompaniment can be indicated and the movements read as if performed.

A few useful symbols are included here. For more information see Ann Hutchinson's *Labanotation*.

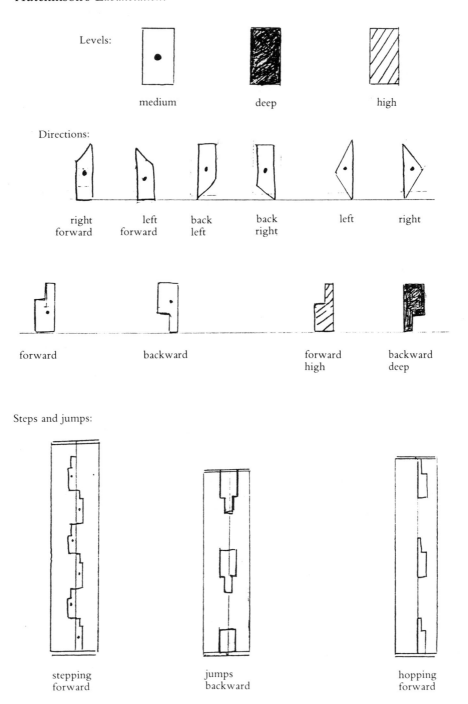

Levels:

medium   deep   high

Directions:

right   left   back   back   left   right
forward   forward   left   right

forward   backward   forward   backward
                                    high   deep

Steps and jumps:

stepping   jumps   hopping
forward   backward   forward

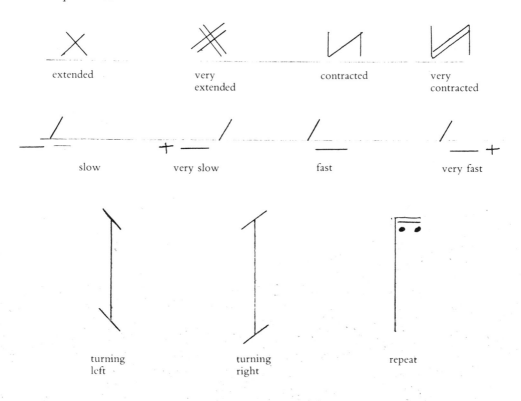

extended	very extended	contracted	very contracted

slow	very slow	fast	very fast

turning left	turning right	repeat

Phrase

A dance communicates through the way the movements are structured in phrases as well as the movements themselves. The relationship between one movement and another, between one phrase and another, brings the statement together. A phrase may be a pattern of related movements or a single movement. Phrases of equal length and stress are monotonous. A phrase of movement can include a rise and fall as in a spoken sentence; an accent at the beginning, during or at the end; repetition; surprise; a logical relationship with the preceding and following phrase; a contrast.

Make a phrase of movement using: travel, lift and turn. Repeat the phase and explore the effect of changes in accent, speed, continuity. Perform the phrase as if it were the beginning or the end of a dance.

Pass a phrase of movement on. The next dancer must add another phrase. Continue adding phrases till memory and logic suffer!

Posture

Posture and alignment are maintained by using visual cues such as the vertical structure of a building, and by the inner ear and the body receptors. Good

posture allows for maximum bodily function with the expenditure of the least energy.

The feet provide a very small base of support of the upright body which strives to offset the gravitational pull. The most stable position is alignment over the base of support and the body weight should be equally supported over the feet over which sit the ankles, the leg, pelvis, back, shoulders and head making a vertical line.

In a good posture the whole skeleton is held in alignment and the body is ready to move in any direction. It is thinking tall.

Except in those children who need some kind of correction, posture training is unnecessary in the primary school. The effect of good or poor body line, balance, and management will be pointed out as it occurs in a lesson, although a workshop on posture might preceed a lesson that makes particular use of alignment and balance.

Realism

Reproducing objects, events, or situations as they really are or as they appear. All art has a degree of abstraction but it may resemble reality very closely. An expression of reality is an abstraction from reality involving formulating and the management of media. Children imitating mouse-like or sea-like movements are not BEING mice or waves, but using movement qualities associated with mouse-like or sea-like ideas.

Rhythm

The organization of time including beat, accent, bars, groups of bars, and phrase.

Beat: the regular pulse beat grouped in twos or threes. A beat can be divided into a double or triple beat.

Measure or **bar**: two and three beat groups. All other measures are combinations. $4 = 2 + 2$, $6 = 3 + 3$, $9 = 3 + 3 + 3$, $5 = 2 + 3$ or $3 + 2$.

Accent defines a group, usually by accenting the first beat.

Rhythmic shape: The rhythm created by the rise and fall of the dance. A whole dance will also have a rhythmic pattern such as: introduction building up to a small climax, a repeat increasing the climax, a further repeat with maximum climax, a recovery that takes the dance back to where it began. Prose and plays are other examples of this compositional rhythm.

It is important that children are able to discover and sense their own rhythmic patterns. Too much dependence on musical accompaniment inhibits this.

Self-image

An awareness of the self and awareness of the body as the instrument of dance; a confidence that contributes to a sense of commitment giving expression and communication conviction and validity.

Teaching dance is about developing this sense of mattering both of the work and the person.

Sequence

One movement added to another makes a sequence. Even a simple sequence of two movements sets up a transition and relationship. The ability to make dance is about creating sequences that logically relate to one another and have a part to play in the way the whole dance comes together.

The ability and understanding of a sequence might begin with

   (i)   A still shape A
  (ii)   moving into and out of the still shape   A1
 (iii)   a still shape B
 (iv)   moving into and out of the still shape   B1
  (v)   joining A and B   A   B
 (vi)   composing this sequence   A   A1   A   B

Sequences might contain clear shapes or be more concerned with shaping and passing through. Sequences can be improvised or planned and found by 'listening' to the way the body moves and feels.

Sequences are like sentences in speech and can be grouped together in a 'paragraph' of dance, several 'paragraphs' making the whole dance. The rise and fall of each sequence and each group of sequences contribute to the rise and fall of the whole dance work.

Space

The effect of the body and its movement on space. In visual art a marker defines the space on paper, in dance the space is defined by the action of the body.

Unlike visual art the spatial pattern in dance has no real existence, since it also takes place in time (see Chapter Two).

An example, such as dancing a circle, illustrates different concepts of spatial organization and design: the circular pathway; the body shape; the shape of the circle; the relationship between the outside and inside space of the circle.

Pathway

Movement travels through space making an imaginary line between the beginning and the end. The path of that line can focus on the destination moving directly, or wander as if indulging in the journey itself. The shape of the body can appear to cut through the space, parting it to allow progress, or embrace and cushion the space.

Activity

Observe the travel pathway of people as they shop, work, play, are unoccupied, wait about, fetch and carry.

Observe minibeasts and their line of movement. Follow a snail trail. With a pencil and paper trace the story of a line.

Watch the pathway of: a falling leaf, smoke, a bird in flight, a wave breaking, a sparkler. Look at the outline pathway of a still body shape.

Use these examples as a stimulus for movement.

Begin a movement with the hand, use the flexibility of the wrist and the fingers to trail or steer the shape. Extend the movement adding the arm and then the body. Consider the shape of: the pathway, the body, the action. Pause to review the shape of the body at particular moments.

Visual stimulus — angles and straight pathways. Drop some drinking straws and observe the way the lines meet, join, and cross. Use similar formations in gestures and travel; make a group structure and find ways of moving in and out of that structure.

Find words to describe the pathway of smoke from a snuffed candle or marks chopped on to clay. Look at the lines of: tree bark, marble, draped material, sunlight through foliage.

Find words to describe the pathways: 'waver, flicker, cross, intertwine, etch, trace, part'. Use the words to create a movement sequence.

Investigate the pathways used in folk dance: farandole, simple and double caste, grand chain, figure of eight.

Explore the pathway of hand gestures and the effect on the meaning of the gesture. Try offering a hand directly in front or in a roundabout way. Use the hand to command, direct, invite, persuade, interject, reconcile.

Imagine that the pathway of a movement peters out and appears elsewhere. Begin a movement that is completed by another dancer. Create waves of movement through a group, spread out and increase the shape of the motion.

Join locations in the space around the body using a variety of pathways; change speed and force. Change at or between locations. Dance pathways that radiate from the centre; go around the body; cross through the body space.

Listen to the pathway of a melody, draw and dance it. Use the music to direct phrasing and dynamic qualities. Pass the 'melody' line through a group as wind passes through grass; consider the shape and relationship of the still bodies.

Observe a spider's web. Create an imaginary web around the body. Do the lines cross the space or go round the edge? Imagine a huge web fills the space, move under, around and through becoming more free, or imprisoned. See also Lessons 4, 5, and 7.

Body Shape

A still body, like a sculpture, is a spatial mass.

Body shapes can be found and considered by stopping an action as if capturing the moment in a photograph. Body shapes may motivate movement by using the transition from one shape to another, either arriving at or passing through the shape.

The shape of the body is part of the meaning of the movement and is determined by design, context, and action. Look at the shape of the body as it jumps, rolls, balances. Look at shape determined by the structure of the body, posture, stance, leg support, arm gesture, the turn of the head. Find body part shapes: hunched shoulders, pointed knees and elbows, curved backs, stretched limbs. Look at shape determined by spatial dimensions: up and down, gathering inwards or opening outwards, moving forwards and backwards. Look at shape determined by feelings and ideas: crouched in terror, embracing, accusing, joyful, broken, emerging. Look at shape determined by its effect on the space: to fill, contain, support, pierce, crush, repel, join, separate, divide; being on the outside, being inside.

Look at sculpture. Find forms that: fill space; surround space; open up space; close in space. Look at the inside and outside of objects. Can you describe the function of a piece of apple peel from its shape?

The shape of the hands provides a good starting point: find the shape of an action led by the back, palm, forefinger, edge. Shape the hands as if: in prayer, begging, protecting, smoothing, scooping. Draw the hands and look at pictures of hands. Make a logical sequence of three shapes and repeat the idea using the whole body.

Work with a partner: explore the shape of: four hands, two bodies.

Work in groups: make group shapes that are aggressive; form a barrier; imprison; penetrate; surround. Move from one shape to another in a logical progression. Explore the interaction between one group shape and another.

Spatial mass can provide moments of extreme tension and poignant relationship but the forming and changing of shape is more significant than the shape itself and is an essential dance element.

Spatial Tension

Movements and the shape of the body can inform the space beyond the body reach giving it shape and meaning.

The line of an upward pointed finger can continue into space, like an arrow sign, or like the point of a church steeple reaching into infinite space.

The space between two pointed fingers can create a virtual force that is a barrier; the tension between two dancers can keep them apart, and a movement or body shape can enclose a space without that shape being complete.

Observe architectural features that affect the space around them: domes, spires, towers, gables, arches, and doorways, the shape of windows.

Explore sounds that create spatial tension and extend into space: electronic sound, flute, chime bars, strings. Contrast with sounds that have a flatter and more contained sound: block, drum, clap.

Meet or part from a partner with suspicion and find the position of greatest unease. Look at each other's bodily reach into space and note the most far-reaching shape. How is the projection affected by a broken wrist line, bent fingers, a flexed knee?

See also Lessons 33, 34, and 48.

The Shape of Space

As soon as a body occupies the space, the space is shaped. The body and its movement can shape a particular space or shape it in many directions. 'A whole series of ideas depends on treating the space as palpable stuff that can be manipulated' (Salter, 1977). Look at spaces made by pointed fingers and elbows, by group circles that close in, by an arm weaving around the body.

The shape made by the body is as significant as the shape of the body. See Lesson 10.

In dance performance, the shape of the space is established by the very first movement of the dance, by the place of entrance and by the location of the dancer(s). The audience is given, as it were, the frame and nature of the canvas. The proscenium of a stage imposes a frontal relationship with the audience and provides a performance space that has strong and weak places. Coming forwards or moving upstage is part of the design, a consideration that is happily of little consequence in classroom dance in the round.

Steps

See Dance steps

Style

A manner of dancing or choreographing. Examples are:

Personal style — Martha Graham.
National style — Spanish Flamenco.
Historical style — sixteenth-century.
Cultural style — classical ballet.

It is important that the dancer understands what makes for style. Familiarization with different styles leads to the development of personal style.

The sharing and showing of dance in the classroom is a sharing of individual styles, enriched by different cultural backgrounds. Children discover their own style through invention and the expression of personal ideas. Dance that is directed by teacher or music inhibits this development.

Technique

Technique may refer to the development of strength, flexibility and management of the body, or to an awareness of the relationship between bodily awareness and authentic expression.

Technique is often confused with style or virtuosity. What matters is how the body is balanced, how a movement follows through, the line of the body, and how the energy is controlled.

Generally speaking technique in school dance will be implicit in the development of movement vocabulary and exploration of content.

It is often helpful to start the warm-up part of a lesson with movements that might be used later. In this way the children are given some introductory vocabulary and coaching, from which they can select should they wish. Points to consider are balance, completion of a movement, easy transition from one idea to another including foot-work, extension, and use of dynamic qualities.

Transition

The way in which a shape or action happens. It includes preparation and recovery and the relationship with what happened before and after. Movement has a duration so that the way a shape forms is more significant than the shape itself.

The understanding of the significance of transition in dance might begin by establishing a fixed shape such as in a sculpture or still photograph, and finding ways of getting into and out of that shape. Shapes can be arrived at or passed through and transitions may be gradual or abrupt, or include another idea on the way.

Transitions affect the meaning which can be explored by changing the speed, action, use of body, pathway, etc., of the transition.

Consider ways of moving from: stepping to lying to reaching; jagged to smooth; smooth to jagged via angular; high to high via falling; despair to hope; hope to despair.

Bibliography

ARGYLE, M. (1975) *Bodily Communication*, London, Methuen.

ARNHEIM, R. (1974) *Art and Visual Perception*, University of California Press.

ASPIN, D. (1986) *Objectivity and Assessment*, quoted in *The Aesthetic Imperative*, (Ed.) M. Ross, London, Pergamon Press.

BENESH, R. and J. (1969) *An Introduction to Benesh Movement Notation: Dance*, New York, Dance Horizons.

BERGMAN, P., and LUCKMAN, T. (1971) *The Social Concept of Reality*, London, Penguin University Books.

BEST, D. (1974) *Expression and Movement in the Arts*, London, Allen and Unwin.

BEST, D. (1985) *Feeling and Reason in the Arts*, London, Allen and Unwin.

BRUNER, J. (1986) *Actual Minds: Possible Worlds*, Harvard University Press.

CALOUSTE GULBENKEIN FOUNDATION (1980) *Dance. Education and Training*, London, Dance Books.

CURL, G. (1973) *Aesthetic judgements in Dance*, A.T.C.D.E. Conference Papers, University of London.

DES, (1989) *English in the National Curriculum*. In particular, Key Stage 1, Speaking and Listening. London, HMSO.

—— *Mathematics in the National Curriculum*. In particular, Programme of Study, Shape and Space. London, HMSO.

—— *Science in the National Curriculum*. In particular, Attainment targets 1–6, levels 1–3. London, HMSO.

DUNLOP, V.P. (1963) *A Handbook of Modern Educational Dance*, London, Macdonald and Evans.

HUMPHREY, D. (1959) *The Art of Making Dances*, New York, Rinehart and Co.

HUTCHINSON, A. (1974) *Labanotation*, London, Oxford University Press.

JOHNSON, L., and O'NEILL, C. (Eds) (1984) *Dorothy Heathcote — Collected Writings on Education and Drama*, London, Hutchinson.

LABAN, R. ULLMANN, L. (Ed.) (1966) *Choreutics*, London, Macdonald and Evans.

LANGER, S. (1953) *Feeling and Forum*, London, Routledge and Kegan Paul.

LANGER, S. (1957) *Problems of Art*, London, Routledge and Kegan Paul.

PENROD, J. (1974) *Movement for the Performing Artist*, California, Mayfield Publishing Company.

REID, L.A. (1962) *Philosophy and Education*, London, Heinemann Educational.

REID, L.A. (1969) *Meaning in the Arts*, London, Allen and Unwin.

ROSS, M. (1978) *Assessment in Arts Education*, London, Pergamon Press.

RYLE, G. (1949) *Concept of Mind*, London, Hutchinson.

SALTER, A. (1977) *The Curving Air*, London, Human Factors Associates.

SHAHN, B. (1957) *The Shape of Content*, Harvard University Press.

SCHOOLS COUNCIL (1973) *Science 5–13*, London, Macdonald Educational.

SNELL, W. (1967) *Dance Through the Ages*, London, Thames and Hudson.
SORELL, W. (1967) *Dance Through the Ages*, London, Thames and Hudson.
TRIER, E. (1961) *Form and Space*, London, Thames and Hudson.

Index